CASE IN POINT
Case Competition

Creating Winning Strategy Presentations for
Case Competitions and Job Offers

Marc Cosentino
Kara Kravetz Cupoli, PhD
Jason Rife

CASE IN POINT: CASE COMPETITION
Creating Winning Strategy Presentations for
Case Competitions and Job Offers

Marc Cosentino, Kara Kravetz Cupoli, and Jason Rife
Copyright © 2017 Burgee Press
P.O. Box 60137 Santa Barbara CA 93160

MBA Analytica

Published by Burgee Press, Santa Barbara, California
ISBN-10: 0-9863707-3-8
ISBN-13: 978-0-9863707-3-1

PRAISE FOR CASE IN POINT: CASE COMPETITIONS:

I like to joke that Jason and Kara paid for my MBA by guiding my team to multiple 1st place wins at case competitions across the country. Their coaching is straightforward and practical, striking the right balance between tactical and strategic advice that drove us to blow past our competition. **Spencer Siegel, Trade Promotion Analytics Manager, Procter & Gamble**

Jason and Kara have the top-tier consulting experience and technical knowledge that, in the most literal sense, is a winning combination. The tools with which Jason and Kara equipped me led to first place finishes at multiple case competitions during my time in business school. Outside of the classroom, I was able to use the same tools to secure employment at my target company. Simply put, if you intend to execute the case method well, you will find no better resources than those made available by Jason and Kara. **Ken Miller, Category Management, Amazon**

I have personally seen Kara & Jason's students transform to masters of storytelling, confidently stepping up to present to C-suite executives. With combined experience in consulting and academics, including judging & hosting case competitions, their collective wisdom is applicable in any case scenario. **Lexie Cegelski, Procurement Planning & Performance Management, Anheuser-Busch InBev**

Kara and Jason run top-notch case competitions. NextEra has sourced new hires and strong interview candidates based on their well-coached performances. The highly polished work product and presentations delivered by their case participants are more valuable to my company, as a prospective employer, than would be any job interview. **Destin Cook, Director of Finance, NextEra Energy**

In partnership with the University of South Florida, Ashley Furniture sponsored a business case competition for 5 major Florida University MBA teams and their coaches. The teams were prepared with a business overview and asked to solve for eCommerce related issues that Ashley was dealing with. The University of Florida team (our winner) executed so well that their "solutions" were a mirror image of our business plan and initiatives! It was clear that their coaches had taken things well beyond business planning, as their presentation was boardroom certified and orchestrated with finesse, precision and directive strategy. The students performed like seasoned executives in a very real and stressful situation. It was awesome to watch. **Gene Lunger, Executive VP Retail Operations, Ashley Furniture**

Ryder System, Inc. has sponsored two business case competitions with UF. One case involved addressing the shortage of truck drivers in the United States, and the other focused on deployment of telematics systems for Ryder's over-the-road transportation equipment. The high caliber of their coaching was evident to the judges as the students were able to develop creative solutions and present them with professionalism amidst a highly stressful situation. As an alumnus of University of Florida MBA program, I was pleased to see the strong performance from both the students and coaches as they addressed real world challenges Ryder is facing. **Braden Moll, Sr. Assistant Treasurer, Ryder System, Inc.**

For the past five years, the University of Florida teams have set the bar for the rest of the MBA programs in the SEC Case Competition. All of the team presentations have improved over the years of competition which is due, in part, to the excellence demonstrated by the University of Florida teams. UF team members have consistently displayed outstanding problem solving and critical thinking skills as well as superior presentation skills during each year of competition. I look forward to the upcoming book written by Florida's two coaches, Kara Cupoli and Jason Rife, on the finer points of analyzing a case and preparing a professional and persuasive presentation supporting such case deliverables. UK will use this book every year in preparing all of our students for such presentations. **Harvie Wilkinson, MBA Director, University of Kentucky**

Two years ago, the University of Florida's (UF) team earned first place among a very competitive field at a case competition the Katz Graduate School of Business hosted. The team's slide deck, appendices and performance during the Q&A segment were outstanding. This past year, UF repeated as winners and once again took home the $10,000 first place prize. Although all the competing teams were anonymous during the competition, after watching the presentations, my staff and I were correct in predicting which team was in fact from UF. Clearly, UF (led by Kara and Jason), has a highly effective systematic and comprehensive approach to preparing their students for case competitions. The results speak for themselves. **Joseph W. Pieri, Director of MBA Programs, University of Pittsburgh, Katz Graduate School of Business**

Dedication

To the students who contributed to my experience coaching case competition teams throughout the years. I am humbled by your trust and inspired by your work ethic and commitment. Also, to my incredibly supportive family for cheering me on!

~ Kara Kravetz Cupoli, PhD

To Erin and Kathryn for their love, inspiration, and support ... and to all the students on our teams who chose staying up and pushing through over sleeping.

~ Jason Rife

For my good friend Kevin Corke – scholar, gentleman and world traveler. He keeps the powerful honest.

~ Marc Cosentino

Also by Marc Cosentino:

Case in Point: Complete Case Interview Preparation
Case in Point: Graph Analysis for Consulting and Case Interviews
The Harvard College Guide to Consulting Case Questions
The Harvard College Guide to Consulting
The Harvard College Guide to Investment Banking

INTRODUCTION

Creating Winning Strategy Presentations for Case Competitions and Job Offers

Your team has been accepted into a case competition sponsored by a major consulting firm that doesn't recruit at your school. This is your dream firm and a big reason that you came to business school. You need to punch above your weight to compete against the big-name schools. You need to lead and motivate your teammates. Can you pull it off?

A corporate recruiter from your number one company just called inviting you to a final-round interview tomorrow at 4 p.m. The recruiter is emailing you a case. You have 24 hours to read it, analyze it, and create a presentation for three members of the senior management team. This can change your life and you get only one bite at this apple. Where do you begin?

Why are business case competitions so important? They help teach future leaders how to effectively translate classroom knowledge into positive results within their organization. Going through the process of analyzing a situation, diagnosing a problem, formulating and presenting a recommendation, and gaining approval from executive leadership is one of the best things you can do in business school to ensure future success. You are not only codifying textbook learning, you are also learning to incorporate it with effective teamwork, interpersonal communication, and influence. This is a potent mix of ingredients that enables change in our world.

We don't want you to look at a case competition as a chore or a painful exercise developed by the faculty and staff at your institution; we want you to recognize it as the alchemy that will turn you into gold.

Over the years, countless students have told us that these competitions have been the most transformational elements of their business school experience. We've participated in similar competitions while we were in graduate school. We've seen first-hand how the experience can be a game-changer for a student.

We've also seen intelligent and otherwise capable students absolutely tank in front of a panel of judges. It seems there is a ton of untapped potential out there, with incredibly smart and talented individuals who, with the right coaching, can become superstars. This book will teach you how to take advantage of the experience gained from case competitions, and show you how applying our winning strategies can transform your business school knowledge into career and leadership success.

Knowledge does not immediately translate into the ability to do something. Practically applying the knowledge, particularly when the stakes are high (like presenting in front of executives with $10K on the line), is a key ingredient to long-term success. Can you deliver when it matters?

These competitions fuel considerable learning and development, and success also demonstrates the value of the education provided at the school – it's a win-win. But it must be done well, and that is where this book can help.

We've written this book because students, coaches, and judges have asked how we've trained so many winning teams. We're going to walk you through each major component of our training plan and philosophy chapter by chapter, and we've split this book into two major sections:

> **Presentations** (Chapters 1-12): This section focuses on building a story for an executive-level audience; it's applicable for both case competitions and presentation delivery in a professional setting such as a job or internship.

Competitions (Chapters 13-24): This section lays out specific techniques that have proven successful for creating winning teams. This is geared toward students, faculty, or university staff who are involved with case competitions.

By the end of the book, you should have a solid idea of what a "good" presentation looks like. The real magic, however, is in the discipline of practicing what you've learned. To do this well, you have to try it, receive expert feedback, adjust your approach, and try it again. The more you do this, the better you'll perform.

SECTION 1 - PRESENTATIONS

CHAPTER 1: ELEMENTS OF AN EFFECTIVE PRESENTATION

For the purposes of this book, we're going to use a general scenario of recommending a strategy or decision to an audience of senior executives. The advice we're providing is based on successes and failures we've seen in engaging senior leaders (including Fortune 100 CEOs) in consulting, industry, and academia. Of course there are exceptions to almost any rule (some specifically mentioned later), but these techniques have been proven time and again to be successful.

Before we dive in, though, a quick word about the exhibits. We provide a number of example slides throughout the book to help you understand how you can simply and cleanly communicate some of these concepts visually. As your skills grow, you can create more sophisticated templates, charts, and images. Our intent is to give you a starting point from which you can build.

Presentation Structure

1. Tell them what you're going to tell them.
2. Tell them.
3. Tell them what you've told them.

There's a good chance this isn't the first time you've heard this approach, and there's a reason for it - it works. People have limited attention spans, and executives in particular are often mentally juggling dozens of big problems. Your presentation should be constructed in such a way that the audience can follow along with the story and not be surprised. Surprising your boss or your boss' boss is often a CLM - Career Limiting Move - or worse, a CEM or Career Ending Move.

Here is the overall structure for a strategic presentation:

1. Introduction/Agenda
2. Context/Background
3. Recommendation synopsis (WHAT)
4. Rationale for the recommendation (WHY)
5. Execution plan for implementing the recommendation (HOW/WHEN/WHO)
6. Risks
7. Summary of recommendation
8. Appendix for Q&A

Breaking this out into the classic advice structure:

Tell them what you're going to tell them.	1. Introduction/Agenda 2. Context/Background 3. Recommendation synopsis
Tell them.	4. Rationale for the recommendation 5. Execution plan for implementing the recommendation 6. Risks
Tell them what you told them.	7. Summary of recommendation 8. Appendix for Q&A

Introduction & Agenda

Introduction: For most major presentations longer than 5 minutes, accepted practice is to start off by briefly introducing yourself (and/or your team) to the audience and tell them how you plan to deliver the information. The operative term here is *briefly*. It's a common mistake for presenters to spend too much time on introductions, particularly in case competitions, going into detail about the presenters' backgrounds when it's not relevant.

Your introduction sets the tone for the whole presentation, and you can easily lose the audience with a weak or awkward opening. Gimmicks pop up all the time in introductions; presenters think they need to grab the audience's attention and be somehow memorable. Leading with quotes from Abraham Lincoln or Gandhi and then pausing to let the quote "sink in" has been overdone to the point that it makes most audiences roll their eyes ... and tune you out.

Keep it short and simple. Your presentation should be memorable because your recommendation is well thought out and cleanly delivered – not because you led with an old European proverb.

Common sense applies here – if everyone in the room already knows you, don't waste time on your introduction. However, if you're in a situation in which your personal background can establish credibility with an unfamiliar audience, then you should invest some time on who you are and why you're there. Case competitions almost universally fall into the "be brief" category.

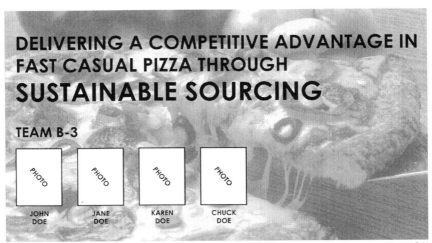

Introduction Slide

Case competitions often have clear rules regarding what should be included on the introduction slide. In this example, we've shown a case related to sustainability for a pizza chain. The slide contains the title, team name, and photos/names of the team members. The design is simple but clean and professional.

Agenda: During the feedback session for one winning case team, a judge commented, "At no point in your team's presentation was I questioning what would come next. Everything flowed so well." Briefly walking your audience through what you plan to cover in the next X minutes lets them know what to expect. At this point, you're beginning the process of "telling them what you're about to tell them."

Best practice is a single slide with 4-6 milestones. If you're tempted to go past 6 milestones, you should consolidate your topics. If you have fewer than 4 items, an agenda might not make sense. If you'll present for just 5 minutes, skip an agenda slide and just get to it. For most case competitions with 10-minute-plus presentations, an agenda is par for the course.

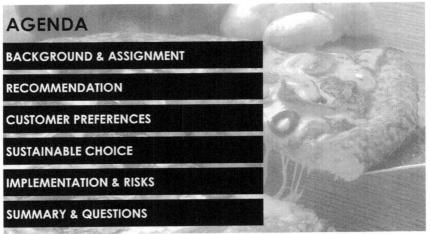

Agenda Example

An agenda tracker can be an effective tool, showing your audience the progress of the presentation.

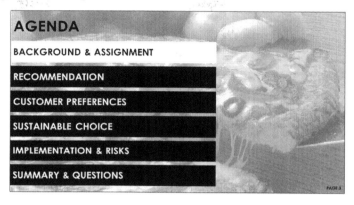

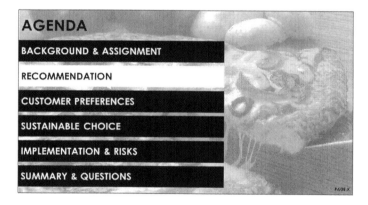

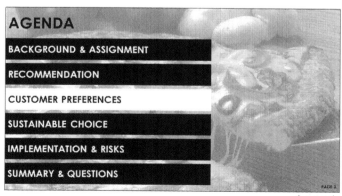

Agenda Tracker

As you move through each portion of the presentation, you can recall the agenda slide and highlight the next section. It's relatively easy to just copy and paste the agenda slide again as a separator, only adjusting the border or color fill of the portion about to be covered. This provides continuity and helps the audience understand where we've been and what to expect next. It is also a great opportunity to transition smoothly between speakers.

One of the themes you'll note in this book is simplicity. The winning presentations we've seen are not typically celebrated for their complexity; they won because the audience could clearly articulate the recommendation in one sentence and then provide two or three points from memory about why it would work. Simplicity is your friend.

Chapter 2: Context and Background

It's very common to see presenters mess this up by spending either too much or too little time on the background of the problem. Channeling *Goldilocks* – this presenter spent too much time telling me what I already knew, and this other presenter confused me because I wasn't at all familiar with the issue, but THIS presenter gave me just enough information to understand the situation without boring me to death.

You get to "just right" by knowing your audience. If you're presenting to a team of executives with an average company tenure exceeding 20 years, burning 10 minutes to tell them about the history of the company or charting how sales have dropped for the last four quarters (like they don't know) is a good way to get interrupted and told to "hurry the hell up and tell us what we need to do."

On the flip side, if you're introducing a recommendation on a subject with which the audience is largely unfamiliar (e.g., a panel of case competition judges that includes executives from outside the topic company), you're going to need to spend a little more time explaining the problem.

How long is enough? A good rule of thumb is no more than 2 minutes of introductory context for a well-versed audience, and a 5-minute maximum for something out of the ordinary before you get to the answer.

If you find yourself in a case competition that has a specific theme (e.g., ethics or sustainability), you should acknowledge as part of this section how your team is incorporating the theme into the analysis or solution.

Sticking with the pizza example, we first have a slide that covers background about the company. It gives us a sense of its geographic footprint and annual sales and shows us that the company is experiencing stagnation after a period of explosive growth.

ABC BACKGROUND

 84 LOCATIONS IN **9** METRO AREAS

 $90M TOTAL ANNUAL REVENUE

 85 LOCAL / REGIONAL / NATIONAL AWARDS FOR QUALITY & SERVICE

 FASTEST GROWING PIZZA FRANCHISE IN U.S. IN 2016, BUT GROWTH SLOWING

SOURCE: 2016 RESTAURANT MONTHLY

2017 METRO AREA FOOTPRINT

TOTAL LOCATIONS

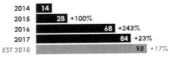

2014	14	
2015	28	+100%
2016	68	+243%
2017	84	+23%
EST 2018	98	+17%

Context 1

Our next slide shows the company's core principles and explains what we've been asked to accomplish, which is strongly tied to those principles.

ASSIGNMENT

REIGNITE SUSTAINABLE GROWTH WITHOUT COMPROMISING ABC CORE PRINCIPLES

Context 2

With just two quick slides, we have provided just enough context for a judge who has perhaps not read the case to understand the issues. We did not go into great detail about the company's history or its product offerings. Unless those components are vital to understanding the case, we skip them and move on.

The temptation to provide a great deal of background to the audience is very strong, particularly if the topic is something you're enthused about. You must be ruthlessly efficient with your time, though, providing only enough context to properly frame the problem and set up your solution.

CHAPTER 3: RECOMMENDATION – LEADING WITH THE ANSWER

Get to the point.

One of the worst things you can do to executives is to waste their time. If you're making a recommendation or asking a leader to do something, you need to communicate quickly and clearly.

Time is precious to leaders, and the good ones have figured out how to cut anything that doesn't add value to their day.

Next time you find yourself in a presentation with an executive and the presenter distributes handouts, watch what happens. The exec will often start flipping through the deck rather than waiting for the presenter to walk through it. The exec wants to know why he or she is there, what the recommendation is, and the potential effects of that decision.

A common mistake of presenters is to take a bottom-up approach. They've been told that they have 30 minutes to present their project to the CEO, who is visiting the division's headquarters for the semi-annual review. Their first instinct is to take the audience through the same process they themselves went through to arrive at the recommendation. The structure goes something like this, "First I looked at factor A, then B, and then C ... then I considered the effects of external events D and E ... which finally led me to consider options 1, 2, and 3 ... then I evaluated each based on the following criteria ... " and 25 minutes later, we finally learn Option 2 is the recommendation.

Reality is more like this: 15 minutes before the presentation, the Division VP tells the presenter that project reviews are running behind schedule and the CEO now has to cut out early because she has to go meet with a major customer. The original 30-minute window is now 10, which throws off the presenter's entire story, and the results are usually not pretty.

Or, worse, the presenter kicks things off and is just 5 or 10 minutes in when the CEO interrupts and says, "Stop ... what is the problem, and what do we do about it?" Again ... these usually don't end well.

When presenting to executives, you need to be prepared to accelerate your delivery and explain your recommendation and the major supporting points within 5 minutes ... maybe even 2 minutes. If you walk in with a bottom-up structure, you're dead meat.

The Top-down approach is what most executives prefer. After giving just enough context for the audience to understand the issue, tell them what you plan to do, and then tell them you're going to explain why this is the right choice and how the organization can make it happen.

This is a very similar mindset to the "wrap-up" or "elevator" question that concludes many strategy consulting case interviews. After going through multiple detailed analyses, you're told that the client's CFO steps onto the elevator with you and asks what you think they should do. You have until the elevator reaches his floor to summarize your findings, starting with the recommendation, supporting it with your strongest points, and then quickly outlining risks and other analyses you want to complete.

When laying out the initial recommendation, you need to be clear on what you're recommending and the effects it will have.

RECOMMENDATION

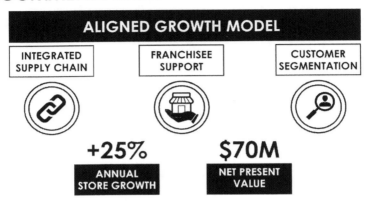

Early Recommendation

In this example, we are recommending for the pizza client a three-pronged approach that will deliver an increase in the number of stores and a strong net present value (NPV). Notice, though, that we don't provide detail on the slide about each component – that would come later in the presentation. We are just explaining to the audience what we are about to tell them. By using icons in this up-front explanation, you can reuse them later in the presentation to create consistent points of reference that will make the story flow clearly.

Exceptions to this rule:
If you are recommending something controversial or something that requires substantial explanation to make sense, you should consider first walking the audience through the rationale or background. If there's a reasonable chance that the audience will be angry or confused if you lead with the recommendation, you should modify the approach.

Sales presentations, whether looking for a quick close or a long-play, are their own animal entirely, so we'll just recommend that you look for expert sources to specifically address that type of pitch.

Keep in mind that we want the audience to be able to explain your recommendation in one sentence. Setting the stage up front with your recommendation and then repeating it several times will greatly increase the likelihood that they'll remember it.

Chapter 4: "We Believe" versus "Research Shows"

You know when you're creating a password for some type of website, and as you type in your password, the site lets you know on a scale of "weak" to "very strong" the strength of that password? Building and defending your case can be thought of along the same continuum. You want to create the strongest password possible, right? The same logic holds for building and defending your case. You want to build such a strong case for your argument that it withstands virtually any attack.

There are essentially three ways that we can "know" things – gut instinct, personal observation, and empirical or scientific research. To continue to play out the password example, gut instinct = very weak. Research has shown in study after study that gut instinct is almost completely unreliable as a tool for making good decisions.

The second way of knowing is personal observation, and personal observation = a weak password. Personal observation is based on limited information and is fraught with bias. The human brain takes in so much information, the brain must categorize information to make sense of all the information. Part of this categorization is evaluating information through certain lenses to create organization. Psychological process protects the psyche, and one result of the protection mechanism is that you reinforce your already established knowledge, opinions, attitudes – this is referred to confirmation bias. Bottom line, the validity of decisions is completely flawed. This is the equivalent of protecting your bank account with your birthdate.

The way to build your case with a strong foundation and ensure it will hold up to intense scrutiny is to build the case and substantiate it with data and information created through empirical research. Strategy is to be derived from facts, research, and data. Data provides both the strongest offense and the strongest defense. Data-driven insights = a very strong password.

Influencing with Data and Examples

In a marketing campaign, it is critical to provide the target audience with "Reasons to Believe." Reasons to believe are details underpinned with data, which provide the audience with evidence that the company is capable of delivering on their promise. Similarly, when delivering a case solution to a group of judges, you must provide data-driven proof that convinces the judges with a solid rationale that they should believe your solution is viable and provides a strategic advantage. Such examples must be derived from data assembled by the team or from valid sources.

Additionally, data and examples must be of sufficient depth to be persuasive.

What constitutes enough depth, you ask? Fair question, but one that is difficult to answer succinctly. The examples and data you present must meet a subjective sniff test that reflects the depth expected by the judges. The challenge is that you probably won't know that level going into the competition. If you don't provide enough data and examples, your analysis won't be strong enough, but in many competitions there is also a time crunch. You can't spend all afternoon exploring every detail of the problem.

You can also think of this like the required burden of proof in a court case. In a criminal case, the prosecutor must show proof beyond a reasonable doubt. In contrast, the burden of proof in a civil case is a preponderance of the evidence, which essentially means *it is more likely than not* that defendant is responsible.

In a case competition, your burden of proof is much closer to a civil case than a criminal case. Keep in mind, when it comes to the real world, the burden of proof is going to shift around depending on the situation and what's at stake. A few key suggestions outlined below will help you stay on the right track.

Steak Versus Sizzle, or More Accurately, Steak AND Sizzle

The steak, of course, is substance and the sizzle is the style. Think about it, you like and appreciate the sizzle, but it isn't so interesting without the actual steak. We've encountered people who say they have emulated what our teams do – and they were certain it would be a winning presentation. More often than not, though, people see a great presentation and think that simply having nice graphics and good, well-rehearsed presenters is a winning formula.

It's not. We once observed a team that, when they opened, you could tell that they were well rehearsed. The presenters had their parts fully memorized, they transitioned smoothly between team members. If they were being assessed only on presentation skills, they would have done well. However, their 20-minute presentation had seven slides ... SEVEN! The team had zero data or research to back up their ideas; there was simply nothing there.

That is all sizzle and no steak, and that loses competitions. We contend that you need the steak *and* the sizzle. First let's focus on the steak.

Research – Using and Citing Sources

There are ample resources available to you as you prepare for a competition. If the company is public, 10Ks, investor reports or calls, and other documents are terrific sources of information about a company – information that will provide you data for your case. Beyond that, you can find quality data and information in the industry's trade journals. Large consulting firms often publish their own research and white papers on certain industries and/or companies. These are valuable assets as you build your case.

Generally speaking, you want to hunt information until you've reached a saturation point – where articles aren't revealing anything new that is germane to the case. When constructing your presentation, make sure you cite your sources, and get permission prior to using any copyrighted material. (TIP: Just because it's online doesn't mean it's not copyrighted.) Make sure to cite sources on your slides and refer to the citations when you voice over the slides. Not only is citation the right and ethical thing to do, it adds weight to your argument.

Benchmarks

You may be able to find examples of firms using a strategy similar to what you are proposing. If a strategy is already showing positive results for one firm, it is likely that it may do so for another ... which is a great reason to not reinvent the wheel! Many companies are relatively conservative with strategy and want to see that something has been done successfully (and yielded results) before they're willing to invest in it for their company. Let someone else make the expensive "rookie" mistakes, then you can learn from their experience and do it better.

A key element in using this information for your strategy is ensuring that the situations are similar – and relevant to the subject case. Be prepared to provide examples of how the situations are similar, and how they differ. For instance, if your client is launching a new product-line extension in a well-developed market, you should be cautious using for your benchmark a successful launch of a brand-new product in a developing market. If you include a slide on how the comparisons were drawn, including similarities and differences, that is ideal.

A great example of this done well was a tryout we conducted in which the case centered on the movie theater business. The winning team pitched a partnership strategy with Match.com to encourage people to go out on dates at movie theaters. It was similar to an existing partnership Match had established with Starbucks that had proven very successful. When prompted, the team had slides to describe the partnership with Starbucks and all the ways in which the situations were similar.

The team also discussed elements that were different and explained how they would address those differences. It showed that the team had not only conducted excellent research, but had also critically evaluated their findings and developed mitigation strategies.

BRAND LOYALTY: ABC'S POSITION

BEST — LORENZO'S

NEXT BEST — ABC

LAST — MAMMA MIA'S

SOURCE: BOND BRAND LOYALTY 2016 LOYALTY REPORT

WHY LOYALTY MATTERS

81%
2016

"PROGRAMS MAKE ME MORE LIKELY TO CONTINUE DOING BUSINESS WITH BRANDS"

LOYALTY PROGRAMS DEEPEN RELATIONSHIPS

Benchmarking

Proof of Concept or Mockup

Depending on your suggested strategy, you may incorporate a proof of concept into your presentation. The benchmarks discussed above are one example of a proof of concept; another is displaying visual mockups of elements of the strategy. For example, say the subject company is a retailer and you identify that it takes eight clicks on the website to get to the purchase page. You have data showing that consumers generally drop off the site at five clicks, so you want to suggest improved website navigation.

Construct an example of what the new site would look like, including several versions to show how customers could navigate the site. Most people are visual learners and will be confident the idea has merit if they see what it could look like. These proofs of concept are a powerful tool when influencing others.

The closer the proof of concept can look to the real thing, the better and more persuasive it will be. Make sure your mockup is responsive, and show what the concept will look like on a laptop, tablet, phone, or desktop. Even more effective is showing several views to replicate how the navigation should or could look. These tactics will show your audience you have done your due diligence.

E-COMMERCE OPTIMIZATION

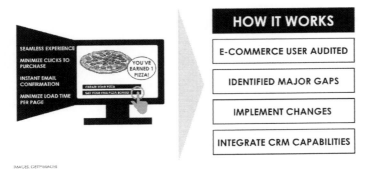

IMAGES, GETTYIMAGES

Proof of Concept

A team of ours once found during case research that it took an average of ten clicks on the company's website to complete a transaction versus the average of three clicks for their competitors. By walking the judges through a brief mock-up of the site, the team showed them how much simpler the interface could be.

We've seen – with mixed results – teams that go so far as to construct actual websites or other functional demonstration tools for judges; they often appreciated the efforts, but because the teams spent so much time on building and showing the demos, the rest of their presentation was sub-par. The goal with this approach is to give the audience just enough of a feel for your idea and then move on. Avoid the temptation to make a really cool widget at the expense of more time explaining why or how it will add value.

Numbers

Bottom line, you must have numbers in a business case competition. This is business, business is a quantitative science, and this is absolutely non-negotiable. The numbers must make sense and they must indicate meaningful growth.

When we say "numbers," we're referring to the financial elements of your case. This includes net present value (NPV), internal rate of return (IRR), total cost, market share forecasts, revenue gain, etc. You will need to show your audience how much your idea is going to cost, and how much money the firm will earn as a result.

We can't tell you how many times we've sat through a painful Q&A session in which a panel of judges absolutely rakes a team over the coals when they show up with no numbers associated with their strategy. It is a fact of a case competition that you may not get any numbers with the case – it's part of the challenge. When the numbers are given to you, that is also part of the challenge. Either way, any panel of judges for a business case competition is going to expect you to provide a realistic financial picture of your strategy. Because, you know, business.

How to Get Seemingly Unavailable Information

Part of the outcome of a case competition is learning to deal with ambiguity. Therefore, it is common in case competitions for no numbers to be included, or for the numbers that are included to be vague. The challenge is to find numbers as the basis for your analysis. You can find numbers for publicly-traded firms in analyst reports, public SEC filing documents, or investor relations documents.

If the company in your case is fictional or privately held, you may be able to make assumptions based on information from competitors that are publicly held. This is an area in which your Subject Matter Experts (SMEs) can provide terrific insights or direction on where to find the numbers. The key is finding numbers that are logical and reasonable – and making sure that you are prepared to outline your process for developing the numbers. If you are making assumptions, make sure you state them in the case and be prepared to answer questions about the rationale for the assumptions.

Moving the Needle

When it comes to numbers, it is key to provide the judges with a calculation of the return on investment expected as a result of your strategy. Many teams know this and will include it in presentations – however, most teams fail to determine whether their idea will "move the needle" sufficiently to make it worth the company's time. We once watched a team pitch an idea that would result in several hundred thousand dollars in ROI for a major multi-billion-dollar company. That company probably spends that much annually on promotional items like hats. That amount is trivial alongside the annual earnings of such a company – and it does not move the needle enough to be interesting.

There is no strict rule that would suggest a specific threshold for ROI that would apply across the board. There are simply too many variables. One way to evaluate this is to do some research on previous company initiatives and see what typical ROI is touted as being meaningful. Another is to do comparisons with other relevant companies to determine whether there are any useful insights on ROI expectations.

Decision Matrix

Another useful tool is the decision matrix, which can take several different forms. They can be checklists or tables – what you use will depend on the problem. The goal is to use 1-2 slides to convey how you decided on your strategy. Judges always want to see the logic behind what and how you chose. What were the alternatives considered? What was the rubric or set of determining factors that drove your decision? There is likely a ton of information and analysis behind this decision, but you will be constrained for time, and the matrix is the best way to convey this info quickly and effectively.

Note that when you are voicing over your decision matrix, you should spend as little time as possible discussing the strategies you did not select. It is a common mistake to want to explain in detail all the work you conducted in order to arrive at your solution, and you will be tempted to explain all the nuances of the strategies you did not pick. This starts moving you into a bottom-up approach instead of top-down and is a waste of your limited time.

It is sufficient to refer just briefly to the alternatives – check the section in the Appendix. You should outline your alternatives in the backup slides and be prepared to answer questions, but these should not be in the main deck or part of your voiceover. Alternative considerations can make for some GREAT backup slides to show off your depth of research. A good rule of thumb is to spend about 20 percent of your time on alternatives, and 80 percent on the strategy you did choose.

STRATEGIC OPTIONS

	INCREASE PROFIT	SUPPORT LOCAL BUSINESS	SUPERIOR SERVICE	EMPLOYEE WELL-BEING	TASTE & QUALITY	SOCIAL IMPACT
ACQUIRE COMPETITOR	✓					
OPERATIONAL COST-CUTTING	✓					
FRANCHISEE SUPPORT	✓	✓	✓	✓	✓	
SHARPER SEGMENTATION	✓		✓		✓	
PRODUCT LINE EXTENSIONS	✓				✓	
EMPLOYEE TRAINING			✓	✓		
INTEGRATED SUPPLY CHAIN	✓	✓			✓	✓
ALLOW MORE LOCAL CONTROL		✓	✓			

Decision Matrix

In this example, you're laying out a list of the various strategies you considered before deciding on your recommendations. The criterion was that the strategy had to align with the company's values (six items across the top). You walk the judges quickly through the items and explain how they aligned (or didn't align) with a particular dimension. Ultimately, you selected the three initiatives that were the best fit:

STRATEGIC OPTIONS

	INCREASE PROFIT	SUPPORT LOCAL BUSINESS	SUPERIOR SERVICE	EMPLOYEE WELL-BEING	TASTE & QUALITY	SOCIAL IMPACT
ACQUIRE COMPETITOR	✓					
OPERATIONAL COST-CUTTING	✓					
FRANCHISEE SUPPORT *(selected)*	✓	✓	✓	✓	✓	
SHARPER SEGMENTATION *(selected)*	✓		✓		✓	
PRODUCT LINE EXTENSIONS	✓				✓	
EMPLOYEE TRAINING			✓	✓		
INTEGRATED SUPPLY CHAIN *(selected)*	✓	✓			✓	✓
ALLOW MORE LOCAL CONTROL		✓	✓			

Decision Matrix Selections

This is done quickly; you don't want to spend much time on what you didn't want to do. If you have specific analyses that cover each option, include that in the appendix in case the judges ask, "Tell me again why you decided not to do X."

In this chapter, we've covered the importance of and how to build your case using data. Data is the foundation of a solid case. First you must do your research, then conduct a thorough analysis based on what the data reveals. Only then will you have the necessary elements of a successful case presentation.

CHAPTER 5: THE EXECUTION PLAN

Many research articles have addressed the reasons certain CEOs failed, including two by *Fortune* and *Forbes* about a decade and a half apart. Both found that CEO's rarely failed because they lacked good ideas or plans; they fell short because they were not able to execute those plans.

Your idea may be spectacularly original, but if you can't explain how it can be implemented, it's spectacularly useless. The electronic and physical file cabinets of the world are filled with presentations of innovative products and solutions that never made it off the drawing board because management didn't think those products and solutions were physically, legally, or economically feasible.

The Playbook

Teams who overlook execution altogether or who just briefly touch on it as an afterthought often find themselves under heavy fire during Q&A about the feasibility of their ideas. During a post-competition feedback session, one lead judge, who was also CEO of the host-company, said our team won first place because we were the only team that provided him not just with a concept but also with a complete "playbook" that he could take back to his organization and hand to his leadership team to execute.

A comprehensive strategic recommendation includes three main elements:

1. Strategy explanation: WHAT needs to happen
2. Strategy rationale: WHY it needs to happen
3. Strategy execution: HOW it happens, WHEN it happens, and WHO will make it happen

The Execution Plan section of your presentation contains the HOW, WHEN, and WHO. We'll break down each of these segments separately in the following pages.

Assess Execution Feasibility Early

It's easy to get excited about an innovative idea and spend a great deal of time thinking about the creative elements and the rationale of why it will raise revenues, cut costs, etc. However, it's *vital* that you pressure-test the feasibility of actually implementing your idea before you invest too much time in the details.

Here are some questions you should ask yourself:

- Will the company managers do something they have never done before?
- Will they be targeting a new type of customer?
- Will they be doing business in a new market?
- Will they need a new sales/distribution channel?
- Will they need a new production methodology?
- Will they need a new (to the company) technology?
- Will this require a merger, acquisition, or divestiture?
- Will this require a significant culture/mindset change?
- Will this require a substantial headcount addition?
- Will this require a substantial financial (debt or equity) investment?

If the answer to any of these is YES, then you need to put some serious thought and explanation into the execution plan. If you find that the company is incapable of implementing the strategy you're recommending without a large investment or a culture shift, you should consider another option.

Of course, if you've been tasked with coming up with a game-changing strategy for a company with an extremely aggressive target or an industry that has been substantially disrupted, then a more radical approach is expected. However, you still should try to be reasonably thorough in explaining how to implement the strategy. Remember, most companies are conservative when it comes to strategic decisions.

Level of Detail

Case competition judges rarely expect you to have every single operational detail fleshed out, especially because you probably don't know the company or even the industry that well. You'll likely have to make assumptions, which may be wrong, but you have at least shown the judges that you thought about the potential challenges of implementation.

The more experience you have in this particular space, though, the higher the bar will be. If you're delivering a recommendation within a 12-week internship, you should likely have spent at least some of that time talking to experts in the company to determine the firm's operational capabilities.

Regardless, you'll be working with a finite amount of time, so as with all of your sections, you will have to balance the level of detail in the main deck versus the appendix.

The HOW

You've heard the old saw about how to eat an elephant – one bite at a time. It's the same with tackling large strategic change.

Key Deliverables and Milestones

What you're doing for your audience is breaking down your strategy into a series of executable steps. You should identify the important "buckets" and prioritize them.

Performance Measurement

"If we don't measure it, it won't happen" is a very common phrase among executives – and it's absolutely correct. Whether it's business, sports, or academics, most people don't perform well if they're not being measured.

A good element in any execution plan is to outline how you will measure success and track progress. Whether you can include this in the main deck or the appendix will certainly vary on timing and the nature of the case and the presentation, but you should definitely mention performance measurement during the presentation, with a slide or two in your appendix that provides more detail.

Identify the Metrics to Be Tracked

What metrics (e.g., revenue per sales call, throughput time) should the company use to determine whether the strategy is approaching the desired goal – and to make needed adjustments along the way? If you're not sure which metrics are important to the company, listen to an analyst call and check out some 10Ks or other reports.

Identify How They Will Be Tracked

Dashboards, scorecards, and stoplight reports (Red – Yellow – Green) are tools commonly used by executives to monitor the health of their organizations and the progression of major projects. If you've never had the opportunity to see one in action, there are plenty of free examples available online.

In short, lay out a simple tracking methodology that will help management understand real-time, weekly, monthly, or quarterly how the strategy is performing.

The WHEN

You need to be realistic and lay out a reasonable path for how long it will take to execute. Multi-billion-dollar, transformative strategies rarely happen in a matter of weeks. Much like navigating a giant supertanker on the ocean, it takes time and a series of discrete steps to enact a change in a large organization.

You now take the critical path items identified in the HOW and put them into an execution schedule. You'll also delineate dependencies here - which tasks must be completed in sequence (A has to be completed before B can start) and which can be in parallel (B and C can happen at the same time).

How much time will each task take? That's where your research and personal experience come into play. We've seen plenty of schedule-related questions pop up in Q&A - "I think you really underestimated the time it takes to do step X." But if you've done your homework, you can defend yourself rather than taking a wild guess and throwing a number out there. This is a GREAT place for benchmark research!

Gantt Charts

The Gantt chart is probably the most common project management tool employed in presentations to display timelines, so it's typically what we recommend you use absent specific knowledge about a company's preferred tool.

Each task is a line item, and the time required to complete that task is represented by a horizontal bar. It's relatively easy to see at a glance the number of deliverables, the total time required, and the relative dependencies of each item.

It's very easy to get carried away and list every single step in the process, but a high-level timeline will typically work for the main deck, and you can include a more detailed version in the appendix.

Following are some examples of varying levels of detail for two different cases.

EXECUTION PLAN

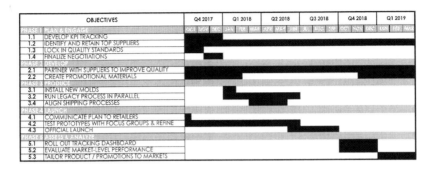

OBJECTIVES		Q4 2017	Q1 2018	Q2 2018	Q3 2018	Q4 2018	Q1 2019
		OCT NOV DEC	JAN FEB MAR	APR MAY JUN	JUL AUG SEP	OCT NOV DEC	JAN FEB MAR
PHASE 1 PLAN & ENGAGE							
1.1	DEVELOP KPI TRACKING						
1.2	IDENTIFY AND RETAIN TOP SUPPLIERS						
1.3	LOCK IN QUALITY STANDARDS						
1.4	FINALIZE NEGOTIATIONS						
PHASE 2 DEVELOP							
2.1	PARTNER WITH SUPPLIERS TO IMPROVE QUALITY						
2.2	CREATE PROMOTIONAL MATERIALS						
PHASE 3 PRODUCE							
3.1	INSTALL NEW MOLDS						
3.2	RUN LEGACY PROCESS IN PARALLEL						
3.4	ALIGN SHIPPING PROCESSES						
PHASE 4 LAUNCH							
4.1	COMMUNICATE PLAN TO RETAILERS						
4.2	TEST PROTOTYPES WITH FOCUS GROUPS & REFINE						
4.3	OFFICIAL LAUNCH						
PHASE 5 ASSESS & ANALYZE							
5.1	ROLL OUT TRACKING DASHBOARD						
5.2	EVALUATE MARKET-LEVEL PERFORMANCE						
5.3	TAILOR PRODUCT / PROMOTIONS TO MARKETS						

Gantt Chart

EXECUTION PLAN

2017	2018	2019	2020	2121	2022
WEBSITE CREATION / WEBSITE LAUNCH	WEBSITE PROMOTION	E-COMMERCE TRACKING AND EXPANSION			
XYZ DUE DILIGENCE	ACQUISITION OF XYZ / INTEGRATE INTO CATALOG	NEW PRODUCT LINE LAUNCH	TRACKING AND REFINEMENT OF XYZ PRODUCT LINE		
SITE SELCTION FOR FLAGSHIP	PURCHASE SITE AND DESIGN FLAGSHIP	CONSTRUCT FLAGSHIP LOCATION	TRAINING / PROMOTION / LAUNCH FLAGSHIP	TRACK RESULTS AND REFINE MODEL	

Simplified Gantt Chart

Regardless of the level of detail you display, you must include some sort of timeline in your main presentation.

FRANCHISEE MANAGEMENT ORGANIZATIONAL STRUCTURE

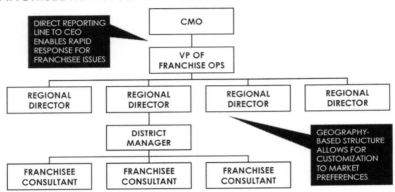

Human Capital

The WHO

Any sports playbook will define and assign basic roles. A business organization is no different. Each organization (e.g., Marketing, Finance, Sales, Procurement, Accounting, HR, IT, Legal) has a particular set of skills that support the organization's strategic objectives. A good operating plan will identify which organizations should be involved to address critical items.

If you find yourself faced with an HR executive as a judge or presentation audience member, you'd better believe you're going to get a question about people and talent. Showing them that you'd already thought of this topic will win you major points, as this area is often overlooked.

In the above example, we're taking the judges through a new organizational chart and using callout boxes to highlight advantages of this structure. Other human capital slides might emphasize training, cultural changes, or internal communication.

It is entirely possible that the skills required to implement one or more critical items may not exist within the organization. If you need something you don't have, you either build it or buy it.

You want to have that talent in-house, so you must either train current employees on it or hire one or more experts from outside the company.

If you're not able or willing to train or hire employees, you can hire someone to do it for you. This could mean outsourcing entirely or bringing contractors into your organization. If you recommend this option, we suggest identifying two or more providers (e.g., Accenture, Deloitte, KPMG), and then choosing the best fit, explaining your selection process in the main deck and/or appendix.

Both options have their pros and cons, which will vary substantially for every company or case. Bottom line – someone has to execute this strategy, and if the talent isn't there to do it, you need to explain where to get it.

M&A-related Strategies

It's worth noting that the Execution Plan is absolutely vital if you're recommending any type of M&A strategy. The numbers (i.e., valuation) are important, but often the benefits associated with the transaction (e.g., cost reduction, revenue increase, operational synergies) are largely dependent on the new combined organization's ability to execute in a timely fashion.

Case teams will often focus on the "sexy" aspects of a merger, like branding, R&D, or cost reductions, but they'll overlook a few key areas:

People
- Cultural differences
- Management integration (we now need only one manager in this group – is that from company A or company B?)
- Physical moves (are you combining locations, requiring 1,500 people to relocate?)
- Internal communication (people frequently worry about workforce reductions after a merger or acquisition, reducing productivity)

Processes
- Merging IT systems
- Procurement agreements
- Sales channel issues
- HR policy differences
- Manufacturing/service process standards

You certainly don't have to go into detail about all of these items, but you should at least acknowledge that there may be some significant operational challenges with any M&A transaction. This can win you bonus points, and we've seen it mentioned by judges as a differentiator in multiple competitions, putting the team who included it in first place over all the other teams who neglected it.

Remember, you want to provide more than just an idea, you want the audience to believe it can become reality. By laying out the steps needed to implement your plan, you will help them visualize it.

CHAPTER 6: RISKS

"Everybody has a plan until they get punched in the mouth."
˜ Mike Tyson

Every plan contains risk, and it's far better to acknowledge risk up front than for your audience to conclude you haven't considered that risk. You should plan to have at least one slide in your main deck that addresses risk with potentially more detailed backup slides that provide further detail.

Components of Risk

Risk can be broken down into two basic components: Likelihood and Severity

Likelihood: the odds that something is actually going to happen. When a thunderstorm occurs, it's highly likely that your house is going to get wet. It's considerably less likely, though, that your house will be hit by a tornado. In this case, the likelihood would vary with geography – lower in Maine, higher in Oklahoma.

Severity: the negative result if that event occurs. Assuming your house is of modern construction, rain won't have much effect. A direct tornado hit, however, would be catastrophic, probably destroying the house and everything inside (including you).

You should balance both of these components when considering whether or how you will address the risk. Sticking with the tornado example, you have a range of options:

- You could build a relatively tornado-proof home, but it would likely be pretty expensive and it would cause you to compromise other areas such as aesthetics.

- You could build a "normal" house with a storm shelter. Still more expensive, but it offers protection for you and your family (irreplaceable assets).
- You could buy substantial house and life insurance policies, paying higher premiums.
- You could do nothing.

Solution Orientation

People point out problems all the time – that's relatively easy to do. It's much harder to come up with solutions, and those who consistently do so will go quite far in their careers.

In terms of presentations, this means for every risk you identify, you should point out steps the organization can take to avoid that risk or minimize its effect. Executives will ask, "So what do we do about it?" You should have an answer.

MANAGING RISK

	LIKELIHOOD	SEVERITY	MITIGATION
FRANCHISEE RESISTANCE			• FINANCIAL INCENTIVES • RIGOROUS SELECTION • CONTRACT RENEWAL METRICS
SUPPLIER STABILITY			• SECOND SOURCE • 30% THRESHOLD • QUARTERLY HEALTH CHECKS
LOW CUSTOMER REACTION			• PILOT PROGRAM • THIRD-PARTY CUSTOMER INSIGHTS FIRM
COMPETITIVE RESPONSE			• QUALITY VS. PRICE MESSAGE • SUPPLIER EXCLUSIVITY

Risk/Mitigation Structure

Bonus tip: If your strategy is risky, think about using a pilot program to test it on a limited scale. This approach enables you to assess whether it works at a much lower up-front investment and, if it works, to fine-tune it for a full-scale launch. This is a very common approach within F500 companies and strategy consulting firms.

If you don't point out the potential pitfalls in your strategy, someone else surely will. You don't want others to think you were naïve enough to assume everything would work out just like you planned it, or worse, that you were somehow trying to hide the risk. Be up front about risk and maintain a solution orientation. The best defense here is a good offense.

CHAPTER 7: TYING IT ALL TOGETHER

If you had just two minutes and one slide to explain your recommendation, what would you say and which slide would you use?

This is the "tell them what you told them" component that wraps up all the information you have provided thus far into a single, comprehensive, and concise message. If your audience members are later asked by someone who wasn't there what you recommended, they should be able to use this one slide to explain it. It's a visual representation of how your strategy will add value to the organization.

Years ago while working for a Fortune 100 company, Jason had the chance to participate in a strategic "visioning" session that was designed to communicate the company's priorities for the next five years. The strategy had been designed by one of the big three strategy consulting firms and consisted of a series of six initiatives.

Each initiative was its own arrow connecting the current situation to the company's future state, and was displayed visually as a shape similar to an American football. It was a simple visual representation of the company's strategy, and it became widely distributed throughout all the levels of the organization. Unsurprisingly, it was known as the "football" slide.

Every time a project or idea was discussed, management asked, "How does this fit within the football?" A single slide came to dominate the strategic mindset of the company.

ALIGNED GROWTH MODEL

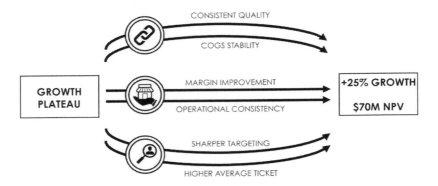

"Football" Slide- Strategic Overview

If you offer multiple recommendations, your slide pulls them all together and highlights how each can benefit the company (e.g., increase revenue, reduce cost).

Reinforcing loops or virtuous cycles are also solid structures to apply to a summary slide:

STRATEGIC VIRTUOUS CYCLE

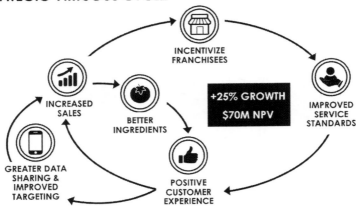

Virtuous Cycle

You should also use your summary slide to specifically highlight the metrics or financial benefits of the strategy. The "prize" number(s) you expect to deliver should be listed multiple times in the presentation to emphasize your point ($70M NPV, 40 percent market share, etc.).

Prioritizing Among Multiple Recommendations

If you're bringing a suite of recommendations to the table, you need to prioritize them. Resources, whether money, people, time, or production capacity, are usually limited, so you should be prepared that you might get some but not all of what you're asking. It's very common for executives to ask, "If we can do only one of these projects, which one do we choose?" You may also get the "Which do we do first?" question.

Regardless, you should prioritize your initiatives and be able to clearly explain your ranking rationale. Depending on the situation and your time availability, you can specifically highlight this ranking in the implementation section or in the Appendix.

By the time you've reached the end of the presentation, you should have communicated the "what" you are going to do at least three times. You should be able to articulate your strategy in one sentence, and your audience should be able to do the same after your summary.

CHAPTER 8: THE LINKED APPENDIX - YOUR MOST POWERFUL WEAPON

This is it - if there is a "secret sauce" to winning case competitions or standing out in corporate presentations, it's learning to use a linked appendix to manage questions. It's the #1 technique you can learn that will immediately improve your game.

Event after event, year after year, judges tell our teams that their main presentations were great, but their performance in Q&A utterly dominated the field. The foundation of that performance can be summed up by the phrase "I'm glad you asked ... "

The reason the team is glad the judge asked is that they have already anticipated the question and have at least one backup slide that answers the question. That slide is kept in the appendix, a collection of all the other research and analysis the team conducted to justify the solution(s) proposed. These slides are kept at the end of the main presentation and often outnumber the main deck slides (sometimes by a ratio of 4:1).

Think about it ... which is a more powerful response to a question? The person who gives a verbal answer, attempting to recite a specific piece of data or research from memory? Or someone who pulls up a pre-made slide that clearly shows the research and directly addresses the issue?

The key is to start thinking about your appendix at the very beginning instead of waiting until your deck's finished (a common mistake).

Building Your Inventory

Odds are you're going to be doing a lot of research, and whether it's reading online publications or studies, reviewing a company's

10K, or having a phone conversation with a Subject Matter Expert, you will compile tons of information to reach a recommendation. Because you are gathering this data anyway, be disciplined enough to capture items for your appendix.

Reading a great article on McKinsey's website about the digital disruption occurring in the insurance industry? Take a screenshot of the relevant section and paste it into a blank slide, adding or even linking to the URL.

Conducting a phone conversation with a pricing expert in the grocery industry? Type up your notes, including relevant quotes, and paste them into a PowerPoint slide. You can come back later and make them look nice, but you're already starting to collect material for your appendix before you've even started building the main deck.

Anything that has helped shape the direction of your recommendation should be captured for backup. This includes things that helped you decide what NOT to do. It is VERY common to get questions about how you arrived at a particular recommendation, considering all the alternatives out there.

This could be framed as a broad "what else did you consider?" question or a more specific "did you think about doing X?" Regardless, if you can show them a backup slide containing data that shaped your rationale for ruling something out, you're going to look amazing. "I'm glad you asked – we actually thought about going down that particular road, but we found some interesting data that led us to question its viability ... let me show you what we found."

Remember – it does not have to be pretty at this point ... just capture it! Better to have it and not need it than vice versa. Even if it's something very simple, like a picture, map, or quoted statistic from an article – save it!

One of our teams, while working on a sustainability-related case, got an out-of-the-blue question about energy usage in Africa. During the course of their research, the team had snagged one of those pictures that shows the entire world at night, allowing you to see the contrasts between lighted population centers in developed countries versus the more darkened rural or economically-depressed regions. They pulled up the map in response to the judge's question and used the pointer to highlight the region of Africa he'd referenced, specifically showing the challenges with energy infrastructure in that part of the world.

The Appendix is also a great place to get detailed on data. We do recommend a more simplified view in the main deck, avoiding the too-common copy-and-paste from Excel approach, which often looks like an eye chart with tiny text and gridlines.

There are plenty of people, though (like finance executives), who absolutely want to see details on the numbers and talk through your assumptions. They want to see how the model works and its level of sophistication.

- Did you account for product cannibalization?
- What were your assumptions for Weighted Average Cost of Capital?
- Did you conduct a sensitivity analysis that shows a range of scenarios and potentially a break-even point?

The Appendix gives you more space to work with to please the finance people without totally losing the rest of the audience in your main deck. Now you can pull in the extensive details from your monster Excel or Tableau model and go through all the tables, charts, graphs, and formulas they might want to see.

If you happen to know a topic or company before the actual case is released and you can run a practice case, you should keep those slides handy for the main competition. For example, you may know weeks in advance that the case may be about Ford, but you'll know the topic only 24 hours before it's due. To help train as a team, you could run a practice case on autonomous vehicles, building out a main deck and Appendix to run through a full simulation.

The actual case may have nothing to do with autonomous vehicles, but you've already done a great deal of research on the company, industry, competitors, and other considerations, so keep that handy as backup. Besides, if they happen to ask you an out-of-the-blue question about autonomous vehicles in Q&A, you've now got some killer backup slides! This sort of situation has happened numerous times to our teams, and it's always fun to watch them try to conceal their glee as the judge throws them the question. "I'm glad you asked ... we actually looked at that and found ... "

Main Deck versus Appendix

The big question we usually get from teams is "How do you determine what goes in the Appendix versus the main deck?" Admittedly, it's a difficult balance and is frankly more art than science. You have limited time and space to work with in the main deck, and you must be ruthlessly efficient to include only the items that move your story forward – don't risk losing your audience.

The general philosophy is to show off just enough research in the main deck to give the audience confidence that you've done your homework and that your recommendation is well thought out. If there was a pizza-purchase study from Accenture that broke down millennials into distinct market segments based on their pizza-ordering behavior, you can list out the segments graphically and perhaps include their top one or two behaviors, average spend, and relative population size in the main deck.

The Appendix, though, might have six slides related to this topic, with details on each segment. Your recommendation could be to target "Late-night Diners" because they're an underserved group and have a much higher spend per order. You spent your time in the main deck talking about why and how to target "Late-night Diners" but did not detail all the reasons the other five segments were not selected.

In Q&A, the Director of Marketing asks why we wouldn't want to go after the "Lunch Cruncher" segment instead. Even though you didn't want to spend a lot of time in the main deck on what you didn't choose, you can now explain that three other competitors are already aggressively targeting "Lunch Crunchers," and the company would likely find itself in a price war trying to steal share in a less profitable segment.

In this case, you had enough data in the main deck to list out the options and explain your selection criteria (profitability, competition) but not so much data that you needlessly used time better used elsewhere (e.g. your implementation plan). However, the material you had in the main deck showed that you likely had researched the other segments in arriving at your decision and was enough to trigger a question that you wanted to get – because you were prepared for it.

With data, you have to know your audience. If you're presenting to the finance leadership team, which includes individuals whose quantitative acumen is high, you should probably plan more details on the numbers in the main deck. However, if you're presenting to a cross-functional panel of judges with backgrounds in marketing, finance, HR, legal, operations, and finance (or if you don't know), you can be broader in the main deck and reserve the detailed model review for the Appendix.

Again ... it's both art and science, and you'll get better with practice at discerning which elements are better suited for the main deck or Appendix.

How Many Appendix Slides?

We always get the question, "How many backup slides should we have?" Standard MBA answer – it depends. The question is how many can the team effectively remember and manage as they control navigation? A good rule of thumb is that you should probably have at least 50 percent of the number in the main deck, and no more than 4X the main deck inventory. Common sense applies here of course – if a company asks you to prepare a one-slide summary of yourself for a job interview, you don't want to give them one main slide with four backups!

It's also important to double-check the competition rules – there are sometimes caps on total slide count, whether presenting or printing. You should always clarify whether a slide cap applies to just main deck slides or includes backup slides too.

One experience we'll never forget as competition coaches is enjoying lunch with our team and a judge as we waited for the results to be announced. Our team had performed very well, but we were still on pins and needles as we waited. The judge was a great distraction to our nerves, though, because he was a retired Air Force general who had flown dozens of combat missions in Vietnam and later served as a test pilot and defense industry executive. He specifically complimented our team's use of backup slides, noting that we were the only team who did it and that it reminded him of his days in the Pentagon several decades earlier, briefing senior governmental leaders.

He said after they finished their presentation, the leadership would start asking questions. In response, his team would call back to the person running the slide projector (back when they actually used real slides), "Pull up backup number 32!" They would then reference the slide and address the question. His eyes then lit up as he told us his secret – "We only actually had about five backup slides, but we figured they'd stop asking us questions if they thought we'd been thorough enough to have over 30!" He then laughed as he said, "But you guys actually had over 30 backup slides – that was amazing. It seems like you thought of everything!"

We won that one and during feedback were asked by the rest of the judges how four people did that much research in such a short time. The answer was that we likely did the same level of research as the other teams, we just captured it and displayed it more effectively to defend our recommendations.

Formatting

The next most common Appendix-related question we get from students is "How pretty do the Appendix slides need to be?" Again, it depends. If you have a lot of time available (like three weeks to prepare a case), your Appendix slides should look just like main deck slides. If you're on the clock, though, in a 24-hour (or shorter) case, content and correct linking come first, with style a distant second.

Material should be viewable on the screen, though, so even if you copy-paste an Excel model into a slide, you should enlarge it enough so the audience can read it. Try to at least get your fonts to match, and make sure you cite your sources at the bottom of all slides, including those in the Appendix.

Linking

You may have noticed we said a "linked" Appendix is the most powerful weapon on the planet. That's because having the backup slides is only half of the equation. You may have 40 backup slides supporting a 30-slide main deck, all of which are very clean and effective. But if you have to manually scroll through those 70 total slides to find the one you want every time a question is asked, it's going to be a rough experience for you and the judges. Many of you have probably sat through presentations like this, watching a presenter fumble through pages ... it's very painful and can erase the benefits you had for even compiling an Appendix.

Giving the audience a smooth Q&A experience is often just as important as providing the content. Being quick and accurate in using your backup slides will make you appear professionally prepared and polished, giving you tremendous confidence that will further improve your overall performance.

The key to being smooth is to create and use a central navigation page and direct links within the deck that will take you to any slide in the Appendix or the main deck in no more than two clicks.

Appendix Navigator

Most case competitions and corporate presentations end in about the same way; "Now we'll open it up to take questions." There is usually a slide dedicated to this that just says Q&A or "Questions." In place of this, we suggest creating an "Appendix Navigator."

The Navigator will include a link to every slide in both the main deck and the Appendix. It serves two purposes:

>   **Functional**: It links you to every slide in the main deck and the Appendix. All you need to do is create a text line or separate text box that contains the title of each slide, and then insert a link to that specific slide.

>   **Strategic**: the Navigator shows the topic for every single slide in the whole deck. Your audience now looks at the screen and sees in one frame the depth and breadth of analysis that your team has conducted. This is a little bit of a Jedi Mind Trick: "These are the questions you are looking for ... "

They also now start looking at all those backup topics. More than likely they developed one or more questions as you presented the main deck. But ... now they might be "inspired" to ask you about one of the topics up on the screen. Which is EXACTLY what you want them to do because it's something for which you have specifically prepared. It doesn't always work out this way, but you'd be surprised how often it does.

Structuring your slides in some sort of order on the Navigator is crucial. You're going to be under stress during the presentation, and even though everything is in one place, it can still be challenging to find the right one quickly.

A good practice is to group your backup slides by topic aligned with the table of contents for the main deck. For example:

QUESTIONS

PRESENTATION		APPENDIX	
INTRODUCTION	FRANCHISEE CONSULTING	SUPPLY CHAIN	FRANCHISEE
AGENDA	ORGANIZATIONAL STRUCTURE	ACCENTURE STUDY	FRANCHISE INTERVIEW
BACKGROUND	FRANCHISEE SUPPORT FINANCIALS	TRENDS IN SUSTAINABILITY	COMPETITIVE MODELS
ASSIGNMENT	CUSTOMER SEGMENTATION	COST PROJECTIONS	FINANCIALS BY STORE
STRATEGY OVERVIEW	WHY LOYALTY MATTERS	FINANCIAL MODEL	FINANCIAL MODEL
INTEGRATED SUPPLY CHAIN	FAST CASUAL SEGMENTS		
CURRENT SUPPLY CHAIN	TARGETING METHODOLOGY	SEGMENTATION	OVERALL STRATEGY / OTHER
SUPPLY CHAIN CHALLENGES	MARKETING ALIGNMENT	COMPETITIVE LANDSCAPE	TRENDS IN FAST CASUAL
SUSTAINABLE SOURCING	CAMPAIGN STRUCTURE	PRIOR CAMPAIGNS	ALTERNATIVE STRATEGIES
NEW SOURCING MODEL	SEGMENTATION FINANCIALS	CUSTOMER JOURNEY	DETAILED TIMELINE
SUPPLY CHAIN FINANCIALS	ALIGNED GROWTH MODEL	MARKET RESEARCH COMPANIES	MASTER FINANCIAL MODEL
FRANCHISEE SUPPORT	RISKS	POTENTIAL SEGMENTS	TARGET NEXT LOCATIONS
CURRENT FRANCHISEE LANDSCAPE	IMPLEMENTATION PLAN	FINANCIAL MODEL	NEW MARKET ENTRANTS
TYPICAL FRANCHISEE PROFILE	TIMELINE		
FRANCHISEE CHALLENGES	SUMMARY		
CHANNEL BEST PRACTICES			

Navigator Visual

QUESTIONS

OVERALL STRATEGY MAIN	SUPPLY CHAIN MAIN	FRANCHISEE MAIN	SEGMENTATION MAIN
INTRODUCTION	INTEGRATED SUPPLY CHAIN	FRANCHISEE SUPPORT	CUSTOMER SEGMENTATION
AGENDA	CURRENT SUPPLY CHAIN	CURRENT FRANCHISEE LANDSCAPE	WHY LOYALTY MATTERS
BACKGROUND	SUPPLY CHAIN CHALLENGES	TYPICAL FRANCHISEE PROFILE	FAST CASUAL SEGMENTS
ASSIGNMENT	SUSTAINABLE SOURCING	FRANCHISEE CHALLENGES	TARGETING METHODOLOGY
STRATEGY OVERVIEW	NEW SOURCING MODEL	CHANNEL BEST PRACTICES	MARKETING ALIGNMENT
ALIGNED GROWTH MODEL	SUPPLY CHAIN FINANCIALS	FRANCHISEE CONSULTING	CAMPAIGN STRUCTURE
RISKS		ORGANIZATIONAL STRUCTURE	SEGMENTATION FINANCIALS
IMPLEMENTATION PLAN		FRANCHISEE SUPPORT FINANCIALS	
TIMELINE	SUPPLY CHAIN APPENDIX		
SUMMARY	ACCENTURE STUDY		SEGMENTATION APPENDIX
	TRENDS IN SUSTAINABILITY	FRANCHISEE APPENDIX	COMPETITIVE LANDSCAPE
	COST PROJECTIONS	FRANCHISEE INTERVIEW	PRIOR CAMPAIGNS
OVERALL STRATEGY APPENDIX	FINANCIAL MODEL	COMPETITIVE MODELS	CUSTOMER JOURNEY
TRENDS IN FAST CASUAL		FINANCIALS BY STORE	MARKET RESEARCH COMPANIES
ALTERNATIVE STRATEGIES		FINANCIAL MODEL	POTENTIAL SEGMENTS
DETAILED TIMELINE			FINANCIAL MODEL
MASTER FINANCIAL MODEL			
TARGET NEXT LOCATIONS			
NEW MARKET ENTRANTS			

Alternative Navigator Visual

All backup slides are grouped on part of the page with main deck slides on the other side of the page. You can also group all slides by topic and just delineate main deck slides from backup slides. It's up to you how to structure it; just make sure that any one of you can find and pull up any slide in the deck at a moment's notice.

Embedded Links in Each Slide

Creating a direct path from the Navigator to each slide is important, but make sure you can quickly get back to the Navigator. You don't want to have to scroll back to the Navigator menu each time you wrap up a question or display another slide.

To do this, just embed a link with an image or object in the same spot on every slide, a link that jumps back to the Navigator page. One option is to create an invisible box in one of the corners that will not display during the presentation, but will change your cursor to a link icon as a preview. Another option is to embed the link in a company logo or page number if you're using one on every page as part of your slide header or footer.

ASSIGNMENT

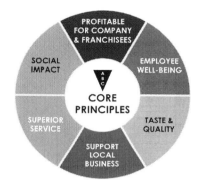

REIGNITE SUSTAINABLE GROWTH WITHOUT COMPROMISING ABC CORE PRINCIPLES

Embedded Appendix Link Visual

By embedding these links, you're never more than two clicks away from any slide in the entire deck. For example, let's say a judge starts her question by asking you to go back to the slide (perhaps number 10 of your 30 main-deck slides) you displayed earlier listing different market segments. She then asks you, "There are six segments up here. Can you tell me how you decided Late Nighters was better than Lunch Crunchers?"

When she asks you to pull up that slide, you simply click on the link, which takes you directly to that slide. After she asks the question, you just click the pizza icon – or whichever element you are using on all slides for your "back to menu" link or "back to Navigator" link. You then select the first segmentation slide that contains more details about the Lunch Cruncher profile. You explain what this segment looks like and compare their lower relative spend profile with that of the Late Nighters.

Clicking your linked icon again, you return to the Navigator (your slide TOC) and then click on your competitive analysis backup slide that demonstrates how the segments are targeted, clearly showing her that three major competitors are already targeting these customers; they own most of the market share. Returning to your Navigator slide, you can move to a slide referencing an Accenture study on the margin advantages a company can capture by locking up a segment versus fighting it out with one or more established players. After you wrap up that question, just click the pizza icon once more and return to your Navigator, ready to field the next question.

And THAT is how you handle Q&A with a Linked Appendix!

If you take nothing else from this book, just consider adopting this technique. Anticipating questions and having analysis ready to support your recommendations makes you look like a serious professional. Learn how to do this, practice it, apply it.

CHAPTER 9: STORYBOARDING

The key point of this chapter is that you must think of your presentation as a story. Storytelling is a powerful way to communicate a message and have it "stick" with the audience. Teaching our students to tell an effective story – and to structure their presentations as stories – has been a key factor in winning.

The elements of storytelling are:

- Understanding your audience
- Using visualization to map your story (storyboarding)
- Ensuring that your story is linear (*Pulp Fiction* made a good movie, but isn't the way to win a case competition)
- Making sure you have some time for iteration

Understanding Your Audience

Any story you tell starts with the audience. They are the most important factor, particularly when you want to persuade them to select your idea as the best. Ask yourself, what is important to the judges? What positions do they hold in the organization, what is their focus?

We attended a competition in which the subject company was Anheuser Busch. All the judges were from the entertainment division (either Sea World or Busch Gardens). Most of the teams focused on the beer business, and only one team focused on the entertainment side of the business. Guess which team won? The one that focused on the entertainment side.

Judge are human – they have biases, and you must pay attention to and address these biases to ensure you are heard. If you don't know much about the judges, you should include the key functions of a company and how your strategy relates to each of those functions.

Even if your strategy is heavily based in marketing, it is essential that you weave the financial, operational, and human capital aspects of the strategy into your story to capture the attention of your audience.

If the case is a live one (current problem faced by a real company), you have the added opportunity of researching the culture of the organization to determine the key values and drivers of the company. For example, most consumer products and goods (CPG) firms are driven by their marketing. Your story should focus heavily on marketing aspects of your strategy, otherwise the audience may conclude that you don't really have a good understanding of what it takes to create a successful strategy.

Assuming the company is public, listening to recordings of investor calls, reading financial documents, and reviewing posted materials from investor relations websites will give you clues into what is important to a company. Once you know that, you'll know key elements of the culture and values of the organization that will help you frame your story.

Laying It Out: Using Visualization to Map Your Story

One way to build a clear story is to write down the key components of the story, one page per component. From there, you arrange the order in which the story should unfold for your audience.

Flow and Order

Story flow is critical. Good story flow is the vehicle through which your solution will be easily consumed by your audience. There is a funny South Park episode called "The Stick of Truth: Underpants Gnomes." In the episode, the Underpants Gnomes describe their business plan for making a profit. It is a great visual for what a disjointed story looks like to your audience.

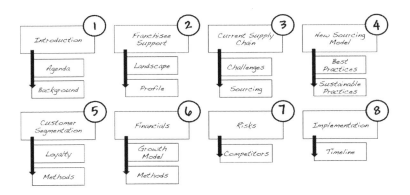

Storyboarding

If your story is poorly structured, your audience will be confused, and if your audience is confused, they won't "get" your idea, if they don't "get" your idea, you lose. It doesn't matter if your solution is the best one, because your audience won't know what it is. Therefore, you must craft a cohesive story that is easily digestible by your audience. Time goes very quickly during these competitions. You will be tempted to think you need to sacrifice time spent on the story for other elements, but do not fall into this trap. Make sure you have enough time to dedicate to thoughtful story construction and you'll be successful.

We refer to this as "connecting the dots." Your team is responsible for connecting the dots for the judges. This is how we teach students to tell a story for an interview. You don't want the judges to have to think too hard to understand the connection between your strategy and a positive outcome. You must articulate *how and why* your idea will lead to results.

In the "Underpants Gnomes" episode, the gnomes think they can steal underpants and then make money. The key questions are: why is anyone going to want these stolen undergarments? What makes you think that anyone is interested in stolen (used) underpants? What is the market? Who is the consumer? How much are these individuals willing to pay for stolen underpants? What is the distribution channel for the underpants? Will you sell them at school? On social media? In an alley? These are the "dots" in business and you want to your audience to be able to understand exactly how your strategy will work by connecting the idea to results – clearly, logically, and rationally.

The main characters question the gnomes about their business model and receive the following:

> **Step 1: Steal underpants**
> **Step 2: ???**
> **Step 3: Profit**

It's VERY important that you have a Step 2 and can explain it to your audience.

You can often see the Underpants Gnomes mindset in action with online marketing strategies. Presenters highlight how this campaign should generate a certain number of views or website traffic (Step 1), and then show the NPV that the project will generate (Step 3). But how do you convert page views, likes, retweets, and comments into actual sales? Just getting eyes on the product or message is not enough – how do we know that these individuals will actually become paying customers? Step 2 is crucial to convincing an audience that the strategy is viable.

The order of the story matters – you need to take the audience through the customer's "journey" through the purchasing process or sales funnel, using data to show the conversion rates at each step.

Once you've thoroughly explained with data how the process works, then you can lay out your implementation plan and the detailed financials. Skipping this explanation will confuse your audience and make for an ugly Q&A session that often starts with "So ... you lost me when you said ... "

Prioritizing

One of the biggest challenges a team can face is deciding what to keep in the presentation and what to cut and put into the Appendix. Some recommend the rule of thumb of budgeting about one slide per minute. Overall, you'll want to spend 60 percent of your presentation time on the details and rationale of your plan. So that's 12-15 slides on the defense of the recommendation and 5-8 on everything else.

Note that all slides are not created equal. You won't spend as much time on transition slides, and if you layer content onto one slide using animations, you may spend a lot more than one minute on that slide. The only way to be sure is to practice the presentation and time each segment to ensure that you won't exceed your time limit during the competition.

Following this recommended budget for slides will help you stay on target and prioritize. When you create the elements on a whiteboard or on paper and lay it all out, what to keep in the main deck and what can moved to backup slides will emerge.

Carve Out Time for Iteration

You'll need to ask yourself "What is central to the story?" and "What can be put in the Appendix while keeping the rest of the story logical?" This is where budgeting time for laying out and practicing the presentation is necessary. You should walk through the story several times; story development is best done via an iterative process, so continue to tweak the story until you're sure it flows effectively.

During the "Forming a Team" chapter, we'll discuss more about team dynamic. Here, however, we'd like to touch on a critical team dynamic that is important for effective iteration and that is *pressure testing* the story. It is everyone's job to participate in the process of pressure testing the story to make sure it makes sense and flows well.

Identify one or two people on the team to play the role of devil's advocate to poke holes in the story, ask questions, and push the team to think about how they have organized the elements of the presentation. This may be a great job for the person you have sitting in the corner doing the financials or it may be better for the person running point on slides. Or both. Intentional vetting like this will allow the team to effectively push hard on the storyline to make sure it holds up to intense scrutiny.

Audiences are far more likely to remember a story versus a set of slides. They will also be more able to follow your logic and understand your line of thinking if the story flows in a logical and rational manner.

Chapter 10: Building Slides

Style Matters

You can have a brilliant idea, but if you present it poorly, the likelihood of getting buy-in is low. We've all seen bad slide presentations at some point, and you just want to tune them out ... or you're just so captivated about how awful the slides are that you start ignoring all the content just to count the mistakes.

When you are presenting to an executive-level audience, your deck needs to be perfect. Because if there is anyone who is going to notice spelling and grammar errors, unit of measure inconsistency, or that a textbox is two pixels too far to the left, it will be an executive. In their own careers, executives more than likely had that one formative assignment in which they first had to draft communication for a senior internal or external audience, and they were probably repeatedly "beaten up" by someone who caught and corrected every mistake. Now they are the people who will spot every weakness and inconsistency.

After listening to dozens of case competition judges deliberate and deliver feedback, we've seen over and over again that it's not always the best idea that wins the day. A decent idea superbly delivered beats a brilliant idea with poor to mediocre delivery time after time. One common response we hear, "Your team didn't have the best idea, but the way in which it was thought out and communicated was so thorough that we'd absolutely hire you as our consulting team. We're completely confident that if we were to work you through the nuances of our business, you'd come up with a brilliant solution."

This chapter will focus primarily on basic design components within PowerPoint, and the next will specifically cover how to effectively present data.

Flat Design

Our teams have used the concept of Flat Design in presentations. Flat Design avoids the use of three-dimensional visuals and limits the usage of colors and font types. The concept is employed in operating systems, websites, apps, and publications including *USA Today* and the *Wall Street Journal*. Here are the basics of the Flat Design approach.

Text versus Visuals - Knowing Your Audience

Much of what we teach students for case competition deck design is to minimize the use of text on slides, using images to support what you are saying verbally. This approach has worked repeatedly well over the years across a variety of functions and industries. However, the "when in Rome" rule very much applies here.

If you're in an internship or full-time role and are being asked to build a presentation for the first time, you absolutely must get a feel for what the company considers good style. Every company is a bit different in what they like to see, and some of them take deviations from that format very negatively. Differences can also flow down to the divisional and even individual level. You'll run across certain executives who prefer a very specific structure for presentations, and you deviate from that at your peril.

We're going to break down a couple of basic approaches, but you should get a feel for what your audience expects before you start building slides.

Visual Focus (Light Text)

You've likely sat through a "novel" presentation in which the presenter is simply reading to you the text on each slide. It's like you're being transported back to 2nd grade and someone has been asked to read aloud. And it's painful.

ABC BACKGROUND

- ABC operates locations throughout the southeastern U.S. region
  - There are 84 store locations in 9 major metropolitan areas
  - Dallas, Chicago, Austin, New Orleans, Nashville, Atlanta, Raleigh/Durham, Charleston, Gainesville
- ABC generated $90M in annual revenue last year
- ABC has earned 85 awards at the local, regional, and national levels for its consistently high quality and service
- ABC was named by *Restaurant Monthly* as one of the fastest growing franchisees in the U.S. in March of 2016
- Growth was very rapid from the outset, but it has substantially slowed in the past two years
  - Stores doubled from 14 to 28 between 2014 and 2015
  - 2016 was the largest growth year as the company grew to 68 stores (over 240%)
  - Only 16 stores were added in 2017 for a growth rate of less than 25%
  - Forecast for 2018 is only an additional 14 stores

Text Light

The slides are a tool to support what you are saying and should NOT be the exclusive focal point of the presentation. The slides should be sharing the attention with the presenter(s).

Use icons, tables, graphs, or other visuals to reinforce the points you cover verbally.

ABC BACKGROUND

 84 LOCATIONS IN **9** METRO AREAS

 $90M TOTAL ANNUAL REVENUE

 85 LOCAL / REGIONAL / NATIONAL AWARDS FOR QUALITY & SERVICE

 FASTEST GROWING PIZZA FRANCHISE IN U.S. IN 2016, BUT GROWTH SLOWING

SOURCE: 2016 RESTAURANT MONTHLY

2017 METRO AREA FOOTPRINT

TOTAL LOCATIONS

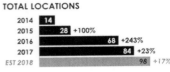

Year	Locations	Growth
2014	14	
2015	28	+100%
2016	68	+243%
2017	84	+23%
EST 2018	98	+17%

Text-Heavy

The whole package comes together as a performance to persuade the audience to support your recommendations. This approach assumes, though, that the audience is in the room to hear what the presenters say, which may not always be the case. This is the approach we recommend for nearly all case competitions in which you present to a live audience.

Medium Text

Some companies adopt a mindset of "I shouldn't have to attend the presentation to know what you're recommending;" they want to understand the full scope by just reading through the slides. It's basically a hybrid between a presentation and a memo, relying a lot more on text to be able to walk the "reader" through your assumptions, emphasize points, and tie insights into recommendations.

RECOMMENDATION

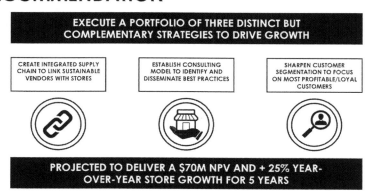

Text Medium

Notice that we're still not recommending you use the Heavy Text approach but are still incorporating graphics, icons, and other visuals. You can still effectively get a point across without writing sentences or paragraphs on a page.

Slide Software Platform or Version

At the time this is being written, PowerPoint is still the standard presentation tool for business. Prezi has made some inroads and has some very impressive capabilities with animation. Google is also gaining some traction, and an html presentation can eliminate software difficulties. However, PowerPoint is solidly entrenched in the corporate world and is unlikely to be knocked off in the near future.

It is important that you know exactly which version of PowerPoint is used to present the slides. Whether we're talking an interview with a presentation component, a case competition, or an actual presentation in a full-time role or internship, you must do whatever you can to find out which software the firm uses.

Going from a Mac to a PC has consistently caused problems for teams in the past, resulting in issues with fonts, alignment, colors, and animations. The same is true for going from one version of Microsoft Office to another. There are functionality differences between versions that can cause similar issues as Mac to PC. We've repeatedly seen teams apologize to the judges for slide errors during presentations that were caused by version differences.

If you did build your deck on a platform or version that is different from what's on the presentation computer, you should at least try to test it on their platform first to find and correct errors. Outside of case competitions, we've found it best to bring the laptop on which the presentation was created (if possible) and connect that to the projector to run the presentation.

Enhancing the Story versus Creating Distractions

We talked about the "novel" approach earlier, which bores the audience to death. The other end of the spectrum is the "circus" technique, which tries to create the greatest show on earth by wowing the audience with a barrage of colors, graphics, pictures, fonts, and animations.

Remember, the slides in the deck are here to enhance the speaker's presentation, not to overwhelm it. The more you learn how to use PowerPoint's many features, the more tempting it becomes to show off, but there is a risk of overkill in each of the areas we're about to cover.

Color

Limit yourself to only a handful of colors in your presentation, avoiding a "rainbow" deck. Clean and consistent are the themes you want to bring across here versus giving the impression that a unicorn exploded.

Ideally, you want to use the color palette of the company to which you're presenting. If you work for that company, this is relatively easy to get by talking to peers or managers. If you don't, you have a few options:

Search for an example – you can search the company's website to see whether they have any presentations posted. The CEO's annual report to shareholders can be a great example on which you can build.

Use the eyedropper function – Microsoft Office programs have a useful "eyedropper" function that will allow you to identify any color from a picture or object that can then be used as an element in your presentation. Just copy the company's logo or elements from its website into your PowerPoint document, and then use the eyedropper to adjust the colors of your palette.

If you are working with a fictitious company or have a non-company-specific topic, just pick a basic color theme and stick with it throughout.

Shade Variations

Once you have your palette, you can use shading to emphasize differences. Keep in mind that with visuals, variations imply differences, so don't just vary your colors for the sake of variety.

For example, your team may have three very different major recommendations, each of which has three subcomponents. You can use the darkest blue for the icons of your M&A recommendation, a shade lighter for your customer segmentation recommendation, and an additional shade lighter for your human capital component.

As you move through strategies, the colors on the later slides will align with what you displayed in your strategy introduction slide.

RECOMMENDATION

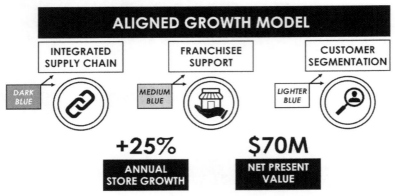

Color Variation for Strategy Components

You can also use shading variations within charts and other visuals, using lighter shades to potentially show metrics with lower intensity and darker shades for higher intensity.

BRAND LOYALTY: ABC'S POSITION

Color Intensity

The point is that you're being deliberate instead of random with your shading, using color changes to support your points.

Contrast

Remember that not all projectors are created equal. Make sure that whichever colors you select, there is enough contrast to ensure text is legible. For example, with a lighter blue box, you want dark text, and with a darker box, you want to switch to light text for contrast. If possible, test your presentation on the actual equipment used, to make sure there are no surprises.

Background and Templates

This one gets a lot of people in trouble when they try to be creative or use one of PowerPoint's standard templates. The risk is that you create a very distracting background, or one that severely constrains you with limited space for text and graphics.

Bad Template

Here we have an example similar to what we've seen on many occasions – a team leading with form instead of function. By putting on a border, they're forcing themselves to squeeze text and graphics into a smaller space, making slides harder to read.

We HIGHLY recommend using a white background for most of your slides. If you're importing objects, graphs, charts, or images, odds are they have white backgrounds. Throwing an object with a white background onto a black slide template just looks awful. White is clean.

You can add the company or team logo down in a corner and maybe add a bar or line that matches corporate colors, but you generally should leave open a significant area of white space to give you room in which to work.

TITLE HERE

LOOK AT ALL THIS BEAUTIFUL SPACE FOR MY DATA AND GRAPHICS!!!

Better Template

For transition slides, openers, closers, Q&A slides, or anything else that has relatively light content, you can get a little fancier. However, you still want to keep the overall look and feel of the deck consistent across all slides.

Text and Font

You need to pick a font and use it through the entire deck. Again, take a look at the company's website or annual reports to get a sense of their standard. Absent any data, pick a standard font and stay with it. And remember, friends don't let friends use Comic Sans.

When we say the entire deck, we mean the ENTIRE deck. This includes all of your charts, tables, graphs, icons, footnotes, and Appendix slides.

Case

You should also be very deliberate in the case that you choose: Sentence case, ALL CAPS, or SMALL CAPS. Whichever you choose, you should generally stick with it through the whole presentation. You can use ALL CAPS or SMALL CAPS for titles and sentence case for "body text," but you have to be consistent throughout the deck.

Size

As for font size, opinions vary on this, but we recommend nothing smaller than 14 point. You should check the presentation room if you can to see how the slides will actually display. We've been in competitions before where the throw of the projector was equivalent to a 46-inch television, and even 18-point text was difficult to see from the back of the room.

You can absolutely vary font size within slides and across the deck, but you again want to be as consistent as possible. All your slide titles and footnotes should match across slides, and your headings and supporting text should match exactly. If you have items of equal importance in a list, they should also match exactly. Any variation would imply a difference, so you can vary size to emphasize discrepancies in items (e.g., decreasing font size as items become less important).

Bold, Italics, Underline

Our recommendation here is being consistent and using differences in style as points of emphasis. Remember, we're going for legibility and simplicity versus wowing them with variations just to look pretty. Avoid using underlined text if possible – people often see it as a "link" rather than a text style.

Bullets

Pick one style and stick to it. Because we recommend staying relatively light on the text, we don't typically have our teams run into many issues with layers of nested bullets.

Also make sure you are using the text alignment and indentation functions so all of your formatting is consistent across all the slides in the deck.

Alignment

In addition to bullets, you should ensure that your alignment techniques are consistent within a slide and consistent across the entire deck. You need to decide whether you're going to use centered, left or right-aligned text, or justified text. Left-aligned text is by far the easiest to read. Justified text can present issues.

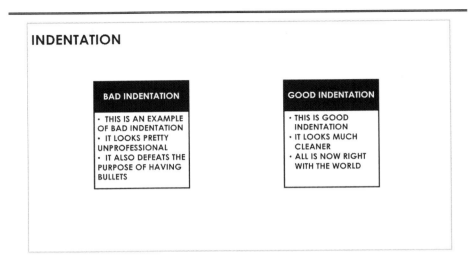

Indentation Examples

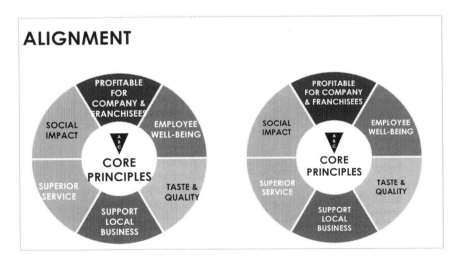

Alignment Examples

The example on the left has text blocks too large for their respective shapes, and they overlap the edges. The right appears much cleaner because the text size is consistent and avoids any edge overlap.

Punctuation

Pick a style and stick with it. If you're going to skip the periods at the end of your bulleted or numbered list items (recommended, unless each listed item is a full sentence, or longer than one sentence), do that throughout the deck. If you're a fan of the serial comma in lists (we are), then maintain its use throughout. Dashes are the same (en or em dash) – make sure they're matching throughout the deck.

Objects

You should maintain a consistent look and feel throughout the entire deck, and the type, attributes, and positioning of your arrows, text boxes, callouts, graphs, and charts should match.

Object Types

Consistency (as usual) is the name of the game. If you want to use block arrows, stick with block arrows. Circles versus squares versus rectangles – pick a theme and stick with it across the entire deck. Your audience should feel a visual "rhythm" as you move through, so their attention can be devoted to the content on the slide and the speaker's commentary. Varying your visuals causes them to have to reorient every time you put up a new slide, which is very distracting.

FRANCHISEE MANAGEMENT ORGANIZATIONAL STRUCTURE

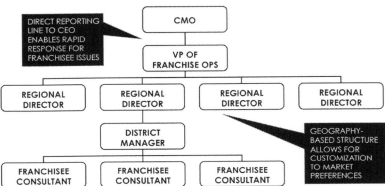

Poor Shape Example

Here the shapes of the position boxes have rounded edges, which differ from the squared-off edges of the comment boxes. The look and feel is not consistent.

FRANCHISEE MANAGEMENT ORGANIZATIONAL STRUCTURE

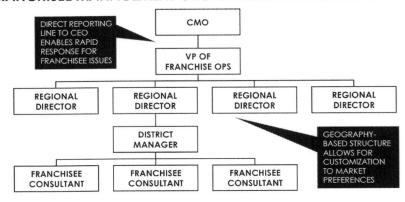

Good Shape Example

Consistent shape edges give a much more professional appearance. It's subtle, but it is noticeable.

Object Size

Differences between objects carry implications. If one circle or box is larger than others, it signals that the category it represents is actually larger (e.g., greater market size) or more important than smaller categories.

BRAND LOYALTY: ABC'S POSITION

BEST LORENZO'S

NEXT BEST ABC

LAST MAMMA MIA'S

SOURCE: BOND BRAND LOYALTY 2016 LOYALTY REPORT

WHY LOYALTY MATTERS

81%
2016

"PROGRAMS MAKE ME MORE LIKELY TO CONTINUE DOING BUSINESS WITH BRANDS"

LOYALTY PROGRAMS DEEPEN RELATIONSHIPS

Good Shape Size

Here you have rating circles that are just large enough to fit their associated text, looking very sloppy compared with the original.

BRAND LOYALTY: ABC'S POSITION

BEST LORENZO'S

NEXT BEST ABC

LAST MAMMA MIA'S

SOURCE BOND BRAND LOYALTY 2016 LOYALTY REPORT

WHY LOYALTY MATTERS

81%
2016

"PROGRAMS MAKE ME MORE LIKELY TO CONTINUE DOING BUSINESS WITH BRANDS"

LOYALTY PROGRAMS
DEEPEN RELATIONSHIPS

Poor Shape Size

This typically happens as objects are automatically re-sized to fit the text within them. Regardless of the text contained within, objects should be the same size unless you are deliberately highlighting a difference with size. You may have to manually adjust the size so it is consistent across objects.

Object Attributes

All of your objects should have the same attributes: corners (rounded versus squared), shadows (off is best for Flat Design), coloring, border thickness (or no borders). This is usually easy to spot within the same slide, but differences often manifest across multiple slides. This is especially true if several individuals are working on the same deck.

Object Positioning

This is probably one of the most overlooked areas in presentation construction but is actually the easiest to fix. If you don't know how to use the Arrange function in PowerPoint to align and distribute objects, look it up right now. It will make your life MUCH easier and make your slides look considerably better.

All of your objects need to be aligned perfectly and distributed evenly. Centering versus left or right alignment of objects (as with text) is up to you, but you need to be consistent within the slide and throughout the entire deck.

MANAGING RISK

	LIKELIHOOD	SEVERITY	MITIGATION
FRANCHISEE RESISTANCE			• FINANCIAL INCENTIVES • RIGOROUS SELECTION • CONTRACT RENEWAL METRICS
SUPPLIER STABILITY			• SECOND SOURCE • 30% THRESHOLD • QUARTERLY HEALTH CHECKS
LOW CUSTOMER REACTION			• PILOT PROGRAM • THIRD-PARTY CUSTOMER INSIGHTS FIRM
COMPETITIVE RESPONSE			• QUALITY VS. PRICE MESSAGE • SUPPLIER EXCLUSIVITY

Poor Positioning

This is an example of building a slide using only manual alignment. It's pretty close, right? And who is going to notice or even care that the objects aren't perfectly aligned? Executives, that's who!

MANAGING RISK

	LIKELIHOOD	SEVERITY	MITIGATION
FRANCHISEE RESISTANCE			• FINANCIAL INCENTIVES • RIGOROUS SELECTION • CONTRACT RENEWAL METRICS
SUPPLIER STABILITY			• SECOND SOURCE • 30% THRESHOLD • QUARTERLY HEALTH CHECKS
LOW CUSTOMER REACTION			• PILOT PROGRAM • THIRD-PARTY CUSTOMER INSIGHTS FIRM
COMPETITIVE RESPONSE			• QUALITY VS. PRICE MESSAGE • SUPPLIER EXCLUSIVITY

Good Positioning

Using the align and distribute functions within PowerPoint, we're able to ensure that objects are perfectly aligned and equidistant. If you pay this much attention to your slide objects, your audience may well assume equal attention in your analysis.

If you have a process flow chart or some other type of visual that requires connectors, the style of the connectors and distance from objects should match; i.e., all should be either touching the edge or slightly offset.

Bringing back our org chart again, this is how it appears when you manually run connectors and don't make an effort to clean them up. Sure, the content is still there, but it just looks sloppy and is easily correctable.

FRANCHISEE MANAGEMENT ORGANIZATIONAL STRUCTURE

Poor Connector Example

Icons

Icons can be a great way to convey messaging and create a memorable theme throughout the entire deck without using text. You can search the web specifically for free-to-use or inexpensive icons, but don't assume they're not copyrighted and just copy and paste them into a slide. Each icon should be intuitive (matches the concept it represents) and should be used consistently throughout the deck. Don't use two or three different icons in the presentation to represent a customer, which essentially defeats the purpose of using an icon.

The look and feel of your icons should be consistent as with all other objects. A best practice we've found is to embed an icon within a shape and make sure all the other shapes are the same size. This avoids trying to estimate the size of icons that may have very different shapes. Just ensure that the icon is centered vertically and horizontally within the shape. And of course, be consistent with your shapes throughout the deck.

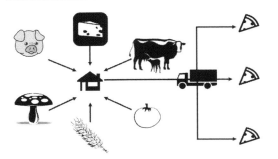

Poor Icons

Seriously, we've seen worse. This is an attempt at using icons that has gone horribly wrong because the styles and sizes are inconsistent, and several of them are not at all appropriate for a professional presentation. Here's a better try:

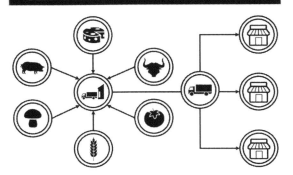

Better Icons

Style is much more consistent, and the integration into the circle enables identical sizing throughout the page (and the rest of the deck).

Pictures

If a picture is worth a thousand words, make sure those words are positive! Displaying pictures is another area of low-hanging fruit in that it is often done poorly but is very easy to fix.

A picture should be purposeful in matching the story you are telling and the overall design theme. If there is any doubt about whether a particular image might offend, confuse, or distract the audience, find something else!

The web makes it easy to find pictures, but you want to ensure a picture is of high enough resolution not to appear pixelated or blurry when enlarged on a presentation screen. Set your web search parameters to filter for large images so you can get a good resolution. File size can be a challenge, but PowerPoint will allow you to adjust down the resolution and remove cropped areas, which can cut down the overall file size and therefore load time.

IMPORTANT NOTE ON COMPANY LOGOS – If you are going to use a company's logo, make VERY sure you have permission to do so and that the version you are using is the most up-to-date. One of our teams received some constructive feedback during a debrief session about using an older version of a professional sports league's logo. There were very minute differences that would be completely overlooked by 95 percent of the population, but the CEO of that organization definitely caught it and pointed it out to our team.

If your team is permitted or required to include team members' photos on the title slide, make sure the images are professional and consistent (i.e., all are headshots from the same distance with the same background). Best practice for schools is to have a professional photographer take pictures in advance. You should also avoid wearing school colors or any lapel pins that could breach team anonymity.

Animation

If there is anything overdone in PowerPoint presentations, it's animation. Flying textboxes, slides dissolving into one another during transitions, bouncing circles, and spinning bullets will make you seem like an amateur and significantly undermine your credibility. Animation can, though, be useful in pacing your story, emphasizing points, and displaying complex concepts.

Rather than displaying an entire slide at once, you can use animation to cause elements of the slide to appear or disappear in sync with the presenter's voiceover. Stick with a short fade or appear/disappear when applied to type or text. This draws the viewers' eyes to the slide as new items appear, allowing the presenter (if needed) to quickly glance at the slide for a cue. If displaying the whole slide at once, any glances back by the presenter at the slide may be perceived as "reading" the slides or not knowing the content.

Best practice is to wait until all the content is edited and approved before adding animation, as changing items after the fact can put the animation out of order or result in missed objects. ALWAYS test your animations thoroughly in presentation mode before you submit your final deck.

A book is a challenging medium to teach techniques for using PowerPoint to tell a story. Workshops, online videos, and one-on-one demonstrations are the best approaches, and we encourage you to find additional instruction to learn the program's capabilities.

Audio and Video

This one is relatively simple. Unless you REALLY need sound and video in your case presentation, you should avoid it. It automatically adds another layer of technical complexity; you must ensure the speakers work and that the volume is right for the audience.

Embedded audio or video should be used very purposefully and only in cases in which you cannot easily explain a concept verbally or graphically. Remember that you are on a tight timeline in the presentation, so clips should be very short.

We've seen case teams make their own videos and attempt to integrate them into the presentation. Not one of those teams won, and they all spent significant time shooting and editing the video. It's rarely an effective use of your time, and the production quality is likely to be amateur.

Do NOT add sound effects to animations – period. It's cheesy and people will laugh at you.

Printing

Some competitions permit or even require teams to print handouts of slides for the judges. Here are a few tips:

- Be very clear about who is responsible for printing slides. If it's the team, then include ample time for printing in your schedule.

- Also make sure you have a conversation with your coach or advisor about who is responsible for paying for printing. You don't want to get into a situation where you've paid $400 for a full color printed handout only to learn that the school won't reimburse you.

- If you layer objects and use animation such that a printed slide will look garbled, you may have the option (confirm with the organizers) of creating a separate print file as a flattened image.

- If printing will be done in black-and-white or grayscale, be sure you use the View Grayscale or Black and White function to ensure the contrast is good. Not doing so may result in illegible text (e.g., black on black, white on white, or gray on gray).

- Binding looks nice but can be expensive – shop around to see if you can find a good deal. Black and white can save you money, but color looks sharp – and you get what you pay for.

- If you're in a 24-hour case and have to print your own materials, try to talk to the print shop manager before the competition, explaining your situation and deadline. That way, you won't roll in at 5 a.m. to find that they're tied up with a big job and can't process yours for three more hours.

We've covered a lot of ground in this chapter, but the key point is attention to detail when dealing with senior executives. If your presentation is sloppy, they're going to assume your analysis is sloppy and will poke holes in all your recommendations to find the flaws they suspect are there – not a pleasant experience.

CHAPTER 11: DISPLAYING DATA

Hopefully, by now we've driven home the point about defending your recommendation with numbers. Having solid numbers is just half the battle, though. You must be able to display the information so it supports your story and does not lose your audience.

Seriously, if you can learn to translate complex quantitative analysis into a simple message, you're going to go very far. The world is full of smart people who can do math, but it is rare to find a person who can do the math correctly *and then effectively explain it* to someone who cannot do the math. Making the complex easy is a valuable skill.

When you're designing a slide that displays data, start by writing down (or typing) the single-sentence message that you want the audience to understand.

We've all seen the financial model that was copied and pasted straight from Excel into the slide, forcing the audience to squint and search for numbers. This is a great way to lose your audience, and it just does not look professional.

The temptation when making data-heavy slides is to dump everything on the page to show that you've truly "done the math" and to enable you to walk the audience through each step to prove your calculations are correct. The result, though, is often a disaster.

This format requires a lot of explanation on the part of the presenter and a great deal of patience on the part of the audience.

How can you have your cake and eat it too? Use the Appendix – it can contain all the details you need to back up your analysis and recommendations. The main deck slides should be more streamlined, adhering to the 4 C's.

The 4 C's of Displaying Data

Clear: The data must be legible and easy to follow, even for those at the back of the room. This means font size and spacing of graphics and text must be sufficient, limiting the data you show to only the most crucial elements.

Clean: The rules we discussed in the prior chapter for object size, color, alignment, etc. all apply to charts, tables, and graphs. Everything should be aligned and "pretty."

Consistent: The way you display the data has to be consistent throughout the slide and the entire deck. Units of measure ($M versus $MM versus million) and decimal points should remain the same and should be as concise as possible for sake of easy recall.

A capital cost of $10,189,065 should be $10.2M every single time it is listed in the deck. Don't list the full number on one slide, a $10.2M value on another, and a $10.189 million value on a third, as we've often seen presenters do. And – even more common – do not use $10.2 million dollars. It's the dollar sign OR the word dollars but not both. Consistency will keep the audience on the same page and make for an easier Q&A as the audience can ask, "Can you go into more detail on the ten-point-two number you showed." To which you can reply, "Sure ... I'm glad you asked ... " and pull up the appropriate Appendix slide.

Callout: Audiences are lazy – don't make them work to understand the insight you want them to take from the visualization of the data. Tell them outright! Calculate the average growth rate for them, show them the basis points, or tell them they must be #2 in market share for the investment to pay off. Use a text box, callout box, icon, arrow, or some other graphic to highlight the portion of the visual that they need to see to understand the story. Animation can be particularly useful for callouts – display the data at the front and then animate the callout portion as you emphasize the point verbally.

Here are a few comparison examples to give you a sense of how a 4C-based approach can be more effective for a broad audience:

FRANCHISEE SUPPORT FINANCIAL MODEL

Average Consulting Hours Per Franchisee	40
Consultant Available Hours	2600
Consultant Salary	$70,000
Hourly Rate (Fully Burdened)	56$
Wages %	44%
Markup	325%

	2018	2019	2020	2021	2022	2023	2024	2025	2026	2027
Terminal Gain	454,586	1,039,080	1,501,088	5,025,068	7,070,358	12,138,314	13,316,256	9,660,075	12,450,052	14,561,479
Salary Costs	140,000	560,000	1,200,000	2,450,000	2,990,000	4,270,000	5,320,000	6,610,000	7,840,000	9,310,000
Other Costs	116,321	409,364	911,094	1,772,814	2,398,913	3,107,547	3,900,461	4,779,769	5,747,213	6,814,857
Incremental SG&A	20,719	79,054	178,104	342,263	443,536	601,941	761,813	933,249	1,122,503	1,329,394
Commissions	6,639	30,883	57,660	131,876	175,044	230,627	289,489	354,746	425,551	505,848
Purchases	57,706	333,080	452,385	876,483	1,190,066	1,541,630	1,930,004	2,377,214	2,851,137	3,373,442
EBIT	$109,000	$316,296	$692,023	$1,344,935	$1,845,173	$2,362,071	$3,029,468	$3,721,693	$4,462,629	$5,256,647
Income Taxes	$33,790	$98,052	$214,527	$416,930	$572,003	$738,442	$939,135	$1,153,725	$1,383,414	$1,629,560
NOPAT FCF (No Dep/WC/Capex)	$75,210	$218,244	$477,496	$928,005	$1,273,169	$1,643,629	$2,090,333	$2,567,969	$3,079,214	$3,627,087
Present Value	$65,679	178,102	364,143	661,346	847,891	1,022,900	1,215,684	1,395,631	1,563,854	1,721,432
Terminal Value	$28,642,800									
PV of Terminal	$13,594,006									
Project Value	$22,630,669									

Poor Data Visualization

So here is the classic Excel dump into a slide, which is actually a bit cleaner than many examples we've seen. This is a mess to try to follow and there is a high risk of losing or confusing your audience as you attempt to step them through it.

FINANCIAL IMPACT
FRANCHISEE SUPPORT

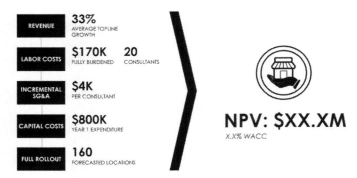

REVENUE	**33%** AVERAGE TOPLINE GROWTH
LABOR COSTS	**$170K** FULLY BURDENED	**20** CONSULTANTS
INCREMENTAL SG&A	**$4K** PER CONSULTANT
CAPITAL COSTS	**$800K** YEAR 1 EXPENDITURE
FULL ROLLOUT	**160** FORECASTED LOCATIONS

NPV: $XX.XM
X.X% WACC

Good Data Visualization

This approach is much simpler – and it's also readable. Using animation, you can walk the audience through each of the main variables that drive financial impact – black boxes appear one at a time (on click) on the left side of the screen, outlining your assumptions or calculations at a high level.

The takeaway metric is clearly displayed on the right side of the page and is accompanied by the corresponding icon for Franchisee Support that we have been showing since we first introduced the strategy early in the presentation.

You can certainly use a more detailed view in the Appendix, but an approach like this in the main deck will be considerably easier to follow for audiences not as well-versed in finance.

FRANCHISEE OPERATIONAL OPPORTUNITIES

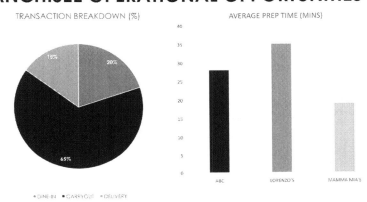

TRANSACTION BREAKDOWN (%)   AVERAGE PREP TIME (MINS)

PowerPoint charts are easy to make, but the standard outputs require design modification to really shine. The above example is common in presentations, but compare it with the version below:

FRANCHISEE OPERATIONAL OPPORTUNITIES

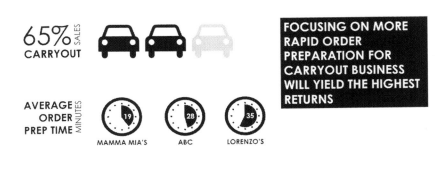

65% SALES
CARRYOUT

FOCUSING ON MORE RAPID ORDER PREPARATION FOR CARRYOUT BUSINESS WILL YIELD THE HIGHEST RETURNS

AVERAGE ORDER PREP TIME MINUTES

MAMMA MIA'S   ABC   LORENZO'S

SOURCE: MCBAIN QUARTERLY – 4Q2016

That is an altogether different approach for displaying the same data. It's much easier to follow, and the implication is clearly listed via the callout.

There are many different ways to display data, and the examples we are providing should be thought of as a starting point. There are numerous off-the-shelf templates that can be purchased or even downloaded for free. A word of caution on these, though – make sure that the look and feel of the entire deck is consistent. A beautiful slide with a complex structure amidst an otherwise amateur deck is a tipoff that the presenter just borrowed someone else's work; this will result in a credibility hit.

Stick to the 4 C's in the main deck but always have the details ready in case the audience wants more detail or background.

Chapter 12: Delivery

There are entire books dedicated to delivering effective presentations. Here, the goal is to point out or reinforce elements of presenting that must be considered when you are practicing and preparing for your case competition. The good news is that you can practice presenting well before the competition and you don't need to know the case company beforehand. Presenting is a skill that can be developed and should be practiced regularly. Whether by delivering practice cases or presenting on any other topic, you can work on key components any time.

The goal should be to emulate and incorporate strategies that will allow you to be perceived as charismatic. Some consider charisma a natural trait, but the reality is that it is a set of skills that can help you be perceived more positively. Below are some key components to incorporate into your presenting routine. Once incorporated, video record yourself and watch it. It is excruciating, but you won't find a more effective way to zero in on your own progress. Second, you'll want to find someone to give you honest feedback. Present to them and record yourself. Collect feedback from both your real audience and the video. Repeat.

Presence

The successful cultivation of charismatic behaviors results in your having "presence." We would define this as having created a force of character through which you are noticed by your audience. While you do not want to be overwhelming, you want to make sure the audience knows that you are there. Think of it this way, you are a representation of your strategy. You need to be confident in it and you need to be sure that this is the best solution – if you don't present it as though you buy it, no one else will. Even if you do think it is a great idea, if your manner is such that you don't command the audience's attention or you don't appear confident, the audience will be less likely to think the idea is a good one.

The goal is to use your non-verbal communication to enhance what you are saying rather than distracting or undermining what you are saying. You must pay close attention to ensuring that the vehicle of the message (you) is as well prepared as the case itself.

Voice

Your voice is an incredibly powerful instrument that conveys confidence (or lack thereof) to your audience. Projecting confidence is one of your most important tools when you want to influence another person. Therefore, it is worth your time to develop aspects of your voice to convince your audience that you know what you are talking about. There are four main areas that, when practiced, will result in your audience's perception of you as confident and compelling: volume, tone, modulation, and pitch.

Volume: Make sure you can be heard. A quiet voice can convey lack of confidence. In contrast, a clear voice that carries to the back of the room compels the audience to listen. In order to ensure you can be heard, practice presentations in a classroom and have others stand in the back to make sure they can hear you clearly. Additionally, you want your audience to feel positive about you and you can use your voice to create a positive association. Often this can be achieved by smiling when you talk; when you smile you automatically speak in a more lively and upbeat tone. Unconsciously, your audience will then perceive you, and your message, more positively.

Tone: A positive tone is a valuable tool to be used in any presentation you give. You'll also want to make sure you aren't conveying negative tonality that will have an effect of turning off your audience. Think about when you hear someone who you find to be negative, whiny, or just being a jerk. Often, this is conveyed just as much by that person's tone of voice as by the words coming out of their mouth. The last thing you want is for a judge to think that you are an arrogant jerk; you should practice speaking so that you sound positive and upbeat.

Modulation: In addition to volume and tone, the other element of your voice that must be considered is how you modulate your tone and volume. You want to practice varying volume and tone in order to create interest in what you are saying. An audience gets bored quickly and will tune out if one's voice is at the same volume and tone over an extended period of time. Watch a few TED Talks to see a good use of modulation to create interest. When practicing, vary your volume and tone in different ways and see what works. Pay attention in class and to speakers, and think about what causes you to pay attention and what causes boredom. A monotone voice makes you disinterested in the topic. The same will be true of your case competition judges.

Pitch: An important area of note when it comes to voice is the dreaded "High Rising Terminal (HRT)." Also known as "upward inflection" or "upspeak," which occurs when a person making a declarative sentence ends the sentence with a rising-pitch intonation, which makes it sound like a question – which is pretty much the opposite of what you should do when making a declarative statement. This is particularly true when you are attempting to convince someone that you know what you are doing. To make it sound like a question makes it seem like you aren't 100 percent sure, that you may be uncertain about the statement. Guess what? Your audience will then question your expertise as well.

Research shows it is more common with women's speech than men's. *Time* reported in 2013 that it is detrimental in job interviews. Social science research suggests that upward inflection leads to negative associations such as uncertainty and lack of authority. Teammates should watch for this during practice and make sure the habit is broken before the competition presentation.

Filler Words

You know, like, um, the words, that like, you know, somehow sneak, um, into, um, you know, ah, your sentences, ah, like, when you're, ah, um speaking. Very little undermines your presence and creates a perception of incompetence like filler words. You. Must. Eradicate. Them.

A special note on "kind of." This one is a killer ... not kind of a killer but a killer in that it changes the meaning of what you are saying. You didn't kind of conduct competitive analysis – you conducted competitive analysis.

Have a friend count your filler words when you are delivering a presentation or contributing in class or at a meeting. It will probably be embarrassing, but it will work. You must collect this feedback to recognize that it is happening, so that you can eliminate these filler words.

The filler words bubble up when you are nervous or unprepared, like an awkward security blanket trying to cover up your discomfort. Become comfortable with the quiet pause while speaking. It is completely fine for you to take a second to gather your thoughts. This conveys thoughtfulness, while the filler words convey the opposite.

Eye Contact and Avoiding Cheat Screens

If you want to engage an audience and encourage them to listen to you, few tactics are as effective as eye contact. Lack of eye contact conveys a lack of confidence. It also allows your audience to detach from you. However, maintaining the right level of eye contact ensures that your audience will stay with you.

But, you say, isn't too much eye contact perceived as aggressive? Yes, that's true, but you'll usually have several members of a judging panel, so you can move eye contact from one person to another. Maintaining eye contact also helps you pay attention to how the audience is receiving your message, so you can see whether they are "getting" it.

What is the right balance? Experts say that 3-5 seconds per person is the length of time you should spend looking at each person. Less than that, and you will be perceived as "scanning," which makes individuals feel like you aren't connecting with them. More time than that and you risk entering the creepy zone. Practice looking at people and counting in your head to get a sense of the time – then evaluate what your natural tendencies are. This will tell you if you need to practice your timing for looking at each person.

Another element to consider is the effect of relying on a prompt monitor. A lot of modern classrooms now have "cheat" screens. These are the monitors that face the front of the room, allowing the speaker to see their presentation in front of them. This was initially designed to help faculty members avoid continually looking back at and talking to their slides (you've seen it). While looking back at the screens and talking to them is bad, facing the audience but staring at the monitors in front of you instead of the people in the audience is not far behind.

You look weird when you just look at the cheat screens. It looks like you're talking to the monitor rather than the people, and it will communicate that you don't have your "stuff" together. These screens are incredibly seductive. "Look at me!" they seem to say to nervous individuals at the front of the classroom, "you don't need to look at the scary audience, you can look at me!"

We get it, we truly do, but we also know that your audience members get it and simultaneously don't care. You are there to convince them that your solution is the best, and part of the equation is whether they think you know what you're doing. Talking to the cheat screens will convince the judges that you don't. You should pretend the cheat screens just aren't there.

When delivering a presentation, if you must refer to the slides, just pause in talking, look back at the screen, turn back to the audience, and resume speaking. As with voice, it is okay to pause to look back at the screen, but never talk to the screen.

Smiling

"Smile and the world smiles with you." As with your voice and eye contact, smiling conveys a message of confidence to your audience. The judges are more likely to want to engage in conversation with you and connect with what you are saying if you have a pleasant disposition. You will be nervous during the competition, so the trick is to smile whenever you practice so it becomes habit.

Body Language

The goal is to use your body and gestures to convey confidence and sometimes to reinforce points you are making during the presentation. More than anything, you should make sure your gestures are not distracting. Distracting behaviors usually include the extremes, either excessive gestures or standing so stiff and straight that people think you might fall over. A few tips:

- Stand "at ease" with your arms at your side (no hands in pockets!) and use your hands or arms to make meaningful gestures when you are emphasizing a point during the presentation. You will be tempted to hold your hands clasped together in front of you. We've heard it referred to as the "fig leaf." It looks weird, but it looks *really* weird if the whole team is doing it. So don't do it.

- Stand up straight – a good trick to make sure you are standing straight is to practice presenting while keeping your jawline parallel to the floor. It helps pull your entire body straighter.

- Work the room – create interest in what you are saying by moving purposefully in the space. The goal is to use two to three spots and move between them. DO NOT pace; in fact you should avoid speaking while moving. DO stop speaking, move from one point in the room to another, stop, then start speaking again. This can be used strategically when you need to take a moment to collect your thoughts. Also, consider the space between you and your audience – a good rule of thumb is about two arms' lengths away from the audience. This simulates a comfortable level of personal space for strangers. Closer than that and you may appear aggressive, farther than that and you risk having your audience less engaged in what you are saying.

- Avoid pointing at your audience or "pushing them down" with your palms toward them. This shows up often in Q&A and makes you appear defensive. This is compounded when accompanied by language like "what you have to understand is … "

Word Choice – Gendered Pronouns, Tone, Formality

So far we've discussed some physical elements of delivery. There are also a few key elements of word choice that are not specific to the content of your presentation, but are still important for ensuring your messages is well received. There are two primary sections into which our recommendations fall: gender parity and formality.

Gender Parity

When delivering a presentation, it is important to use inclusive language. When you exclude "she" language in favor of "he" language, your judges will perceive you negatively. Speakers who consistently and repeatedly use "he or she" are just as annoying as those who always say "he." Try re-writing such phrases, using the plural "they" or even potentially "customers" or "suppliers." Only if there is rationale for referring to someone as one gender or another should you do so – for example, if your case requires customer analysis and you find that 95 percent of consumers for the product are women, then you can say that and refer to a customer as "she."

Formality

While your delivery style should be warm and engaging, you must also be formal in your word choice. *Avoid familiar language, slang, and idioms.* These word choices will result in your being perceived as overly casual or unprofessional. Our "favorite" is competitors who approach judges and say "You guys." *You guys!?!* These people, the judges, are not your buddies, your friends, or your peers. This is overly familiar language.

Slang and idioms are figures of speech in which you use words or phrases that mean something other than the literal definition. Your strategy is not to be portrayed as "clutch" and you don't want to caution the judges not to "cut off your nose to spite your face." If you use such devices, you are going to be perceived as overly casual, or worse – confuse your audience. You should approach them with the utmost respect. This means ensuring your language is consistent with that of a professional work environment.

Google "business buzzwords" for a list of words and phrases to eliminate from your repertoire. Often, when judging panels are making a tough choice between a team that goes forward or does not, they will consider "Who would I want to hire?" and the individual or team that presents itself unprofessionally will lose out every time.

Delivering a strong presentation is how you communicate effectively to your audience. It matters that your idea is well researched, intelligently analyzed, and effectively delivered. All three are important for success.

SECTION 2 - COMPETITIONS

Chapter 13: Forming a Team

There are two main approaches to team creation for case competitions. The first is "dream team" assigning in which a faculty member or program administrator picks "top" individual students and combines them into a team. "Top" may be defined by tryout, random assignment, or class evaluation. The second method is allowing students to self-create teams, which is for many reasons our preference.

The primary advantage is ensuring that the team "owns" the results; the individuals have a stronger commitment to the team because they were a part of creating it. People are naturally more connected to something they have created. Team members are more likely to trust one another, which is a key advantage in team performance.

Finally, we have found that team chemistry is difficult to predict when putting individuals together in a team. Often, these teams are short-term, and there isn't a tremendous amount of time to create and develop positive team chemistry, so it is easier to just allow students to create teams with others they already trust. No matter who builds the team, the elements of team construction are the same.

Skills

Diversity of skills is a must for a winning case team, and the balance of skills may be determined by the nature of the case. If it is a finance case, then you'll probably need more than one finance expert. Regardless of the content of the case, you'll definitely need at least one person strong in finance and one who is strong in presentation or slide development. This is a business case, so numbers matter and your goal is to persuade others that your idea is the right one; telling a story through visuals will be key to this.

Roles

Beyond pure skill and business acumen, individuals on a team will play different roles on the team. In many competitions, effective time and project management is critical to winning. You must make sure you have someone who pays close attention to the details in the presentation. "Okay," you say, "we need a bunch of hyper-competitive machines, got it." Don't forget that these competitions are intense and having people who know how to break the ice and create a fun environment is just as important. The key is to ensure you have each type listed below and establish roles up front.

Time Tyrant

A successful team has a "time tyrant" who will ensure that the team stays on task and adheres to the predetermined plan of attack. Without one, teams can eat into critical storyboarding and presentation practice time by becoming victims to "analysis paralysis." It will be tempting during the competition to want to thrash the time tyrant – that's why you must establish these roles and respect the importance of following the plan.

Slide Master or Pixelator

The Slide Master is responsible for creating the deck template and combining all team members' slides into a cohesive package.

This person – the editor for your presentation – needs strong attention to detail and will ensure that there is adequate time to review deliverables in detail. The editor ensures that each word is spelled correctly, the text is free of grammar gaffes, and that each image is the correct size, scale, and alignment. He or she needs to know when an object is one or two pixels too far to the left and needs to be adjusted for the good of the universe (thus the term Pixelator).

It's ideal if the Slide Master and Pixelator are the same person. If that isn't possible, just make sure each role is covered.

Author

Another essential role is that of the Author, who ensures the flow of the story. This person is tasked with continually reviewing the overall narrative to ensure it is thorough and unfolds in a clear and logical fashion. This person's role requires that they examine the story to keep the rationale solid.

Cheerleader

The cheerleader role is often unappreciated; however, we have found it is central to the success of the team. The cheerleader encourages periodic mental health breaks, dance or karaoke time, snack runs, or activities that keep the team motivated and positive. Research is clear that individuals who are positive and feel good about their work are more likely to perform better. Your team cheerleader ensures that you all stay motivated and excited through a challenging and often stressful process.

Each of these roles plays a part in a team's success. Our most successful teams have been those that included each of the roles above. It is great if your team has individuals who are naturally inclined to play these roles. However, you may be on a team in which each role isn't naturally filled by the personalities already on the team. That's okay as long as you identify people for each role. At your first team meeting, take a few minutes to determine who will take which role and make sure the team understands that each is important to ensuring the most successful performance. You will be tempted to skip this piece when the team first comes together. Don't.

Team Size – Not Enough or Too Many?

Considering team size, we're back to *Goldilocks*. There are team sizes that are too small, and there are definitely teams that are too large. We have found that teams of four are ideal.

Teams that are too small don't have the breadth of assets for the job. This includes the diversity of skills, knowledge, and experience needed to develop the best possible solution. We often see teams make mistakes in the opposite direction, though, including too many people on the team. It may seem that the more people you have on the team, the more people you have to do the work. However, too many people on a team causes problems.

One problem is too many cooks in the kitchen. To some extent, this can also be a personality issue, where you have too many people wanting to take charge. It also means that no matter how collaborative the personalities, you have more people who have to agree on the way forward. Finally, and more pragmatically, the more people you have the more difficult it is to divide the presentation among the team members and still keep the story cohesive.

The Fallacy of "Dream Teams"

Never was a fallacy more obvious than the year that NBA players were featured as the starting lineup for the 2004 Olympic men's basketball team. This was a group of undeniably stellar players, all at the top of their game. The roster read like the who's who of the NBA.

The strategy was clear: put a group of amazing players together on the court and "poof," an amazing team would emerge – just as it had back in 1992. The reality was that this team barely won the bronze medal by squeaking out a win against Lithuania. It was a bitter lesson to those who think that all you need to do is combine highly talented people and winning will naturally follow.

The reality is more complicated – team *chemistry* matters. The ability to work effectively with one another, to rein in your ego and your wants and do what's best for the team, is far more important than almost any other factor in a team's success. Yes, you need smart, hardworking, driven individuals – but they must also like and trust one another or they will self-destruct when the pressure is on.

Coachability

One of the most important personality factors for creating a winning team is its "coachability." The core of coachability is whether players respond positively to feedback and can quickly integrate it or improve their game. Whether the feedback is from your teammates, advisors, coaches, or judges, receiving performance feedback is one of the best learning outcomes of case competitions.

Feedback is a gift, but of course not everyone sees it that way. If you want to win, you need to find people who are receptive to and able to act on feedback. The last thing you want at 3 a.m. during a 24-hour case is a team member who is fighting every piece of feedback received. Watch out for individuals who either shut down, lash out, or blame others with statements like "Well I wanted to take that approach from the start, but they weren't listening to my ideas."

Drive, Commitment, and Hunger

All you need to do here is look around the room and think about the people you most enjoy working with. Yes, it's good to be smart. Lots of people are smart. We all know people, though, who are too smart for their own good. They get bored or frustrated when others don't immediately see things their way. Or perhaps everything has come so easily to them all of their lives that they don't know how to handle something tough.

When the stress and the pressure pile on, who are the people you can count on to push through adversity to do their best? Consider:

- Who is the person who won't settle for *good enough?*
- Who is the person everyone wants on their team for group projects?
- Who is involved outside of the classroom?

These are the superstars. These are the students who will pull the all-nighter to draw the best possible value from an experience. These are the individuals who are intrinsically motivated to perform no matter what they are doing – and are capable of prioritizing and managing their time. Find a couple of these people and you will be well on your way to winning.

We can't tell you the number of times we have been challenged about our commitment to the notion that teams should self-organize. Many will laud the practice of holding individual tryouts and putting together a team of the best of the best. However, we have seen over and over again that the team dynamic is crucial to success. The competitions are high-stress, and team members must carefully evaluate and select the right mix of individuals to ensure a winning performance.

CHAPTER 14: TRAINING AND PREPARATION

We employ the "Train Like You Fight, Fight Like You Train" mentality of preparation. How we train and prepare our students has undoubtedly led to consistent success over the past five years. It is the time invested in training and preparation by the coaches and the students that is the differentiator.

A favorite simile for winning case competitions is learning to ride a bike. You could read a book, like this one, on how to ride a bike, watch videos of other people successfully riding bikes, or personally interview the world's best cyclist. But if that is all you did – just read books and looked at examples – if we then handed you a bike and asked you to ride it, what would happen? You'd fall off. A lot.

You need practice; you need to ride around in safe environments or with training wheels before you really know how to perform. And, if you want to perform at the very top, you practice A LOT. People have told us that they're surprised we're willing to write a book about our process – the fact is that success in these competitions, the part that you can control, is based largely on following the training format we require for our students – and not everyone is going to be willing to do it. But if you are willing to commit, you will see incredible results.

Preparation Process: Learn it, do it, get feedback, do it again, get feedback, do it again.

We conduct a two-hour seminar in the fall to outline our winning case competition components. This provides students with a framework for understanding the "how to" elements of case competitions. This is like learning the mechanics of riding a bike: where to find the brakes, the rules of the road, how the pedals work, etc. This also includes additional preparation for necessary skills such as storytelling and developing good slides to visually communicate your message. We conduct a half-day workshop developing these two skill sets. That is about six hours of learning the "how to" of case competitions.

Preparation also includes acquiring knowledge and feedback about the subject matter of the case competition. Ability to do this in advance while preparing for a competition will vary based on when you know the subject matter of a case competition. If possible, calls with subject matter experts (SMEs) in advance is a valuable part of preparing for a case.

Once you've learned the "how to," it is time to practice. The great thing about the process of learning to ride a bike is that the bike gives you immediate feedback about your performance. You know immediately when something is (or is not) working. The practice cases serve the same purpose.

Practice Cases

Each student is required to participate in an internal case competition, and we conduct one practice case in advance of the required competition. The practice case is the equivalent of riding a bike with training wheels. The case selected usually has a relatively narrow focus and a low level of ambiguity.

We provide examples of good slide presentations we've seen in the past.

The presentation itself is expected to be only 10 minutes, and we draw at random to determine a small number of teams to present. We also provide a scoring or rubric handout to the other students so they simulate judging. All together this provides a more structured and secure environment for the students' first case competition experience. We want the students to feel a taste of success to lay the foundation for letting them know they can do this.

For the internal case competition, the competition itself is similar to many other national competitions – there is a cash prize and executives as judges. However, we do provide experienced MBAs as coaches for the teams throughout the competition so the students feel more comfortable. This is akin to riding a bike in a field of grass. You may fall, but it won't hurt quite as badly as it does on concrete.

Once we've completed the foundation of training, the next time a team engages in practice cases is their preparation for an actual external case competition. Generally, we recommend participating in three practice cases in advance of the competition. The nature of the practice case should replicate the real thing as closely as possible. Therefore, in the scenario in which you receive the case in advance, you should be practicing and refining the case that you are preparing. If permitted by the rules of the competition, recruit individuals to serve as an audience. The tougher and more well-informed the audience, the better-prepared you will be.

The second type of competition is one in which you know the case company, but not the case problem itself. In this scenario, your goal will be to do at least one general strategy case, with the other two more narrowly focused. You can usually get great ideas from media coverage related to the challenges the company's facing, expectations from investors, and other current issues.

The third scenario is the blind competition in which you won't know anything about the company or case problem in advance. In this situation, the goal is to learn as much as possible about previous cases done by the competition to get a feel for the type of case you may get. The best preparation is at least one general strategy practice case and one repeat performance run. Again, the goal is to have three to five individuals acting as judges to evaluate the case presentation. These can be alumni who are experienced in case competitions or people considered SMEs. They can also be experienced classmates, or faculty or staff. You want to simulate the real case experience as much as possible so you get valuable practice and worthwhile feedback.

Time Commitment and Expectations

Our winning teams spend 50-80 hours in the 4-6 weeks before a competition. The 24-hour cases in which you don't know the case problem require less time because there is only so much you can do in advance. The time does add up when you are conducting several practice runs. Add in SME calls, feedback sessions, and other outside research, and you quickly hit the 50-80 hour mark.

You want to win? You cannot skimp on preparation and practice. This will pay dividends throughout your career. You will build an important skill set, and you will have confidence in your ability to produce results during your internship and full-time roles.

Interpreting Rules and Rubrics

These are two very different animals. One must be strictly adhered to, the other requires some level of evaluation and interpretation.

Rules

The competition rules must be explicitly followed – the integrity of the competition, your personal integrity, and the reputation of your MBA program depend on following the rules. Do not ever cut corners with competition rules.

Team Anonymity

Many competitions require that a team's school affiliation remains anonymous to the judges. This is to ensure that the competition is as fair as possible. Take this very seriously. Make sure you pay close attention to eliminating any reference, explicit or implicit, to your MBA program.

Even the small things like school lapel pins on your introductory head shots may get you disqualified from a competition. We once had a team who conducted primary research on their classmates regarding their news consumption habits. During their presentation, they referred to the college newspaper by name, which put them at risk of disqualification.

Use of Coaches

Similarly, the work on the strategy and plan must be your own. This isn't a competition to see who has the best faculty. This is a competition to see which students can provide the best solution and sell it. Your faculty and coaches should not be generating solutions for you.

Think of it like a sports team. The coach can prepare you, and give you practice runs and feedback, but when the game clock starts, the team members are the only people on the field. The entire process lacks validity if anyone besides the team is doing the research and analysis.

Use of SMEs

Just as when using coaches, pay careful attention to the rules regarding SMEs. In a competition, this will run the gamut from allowing contact with any resource (more like real life) to a complete prohibition on consulting with anyone outside of the student team (the strictest interpretation of your team's contribution).

The approach varies with the host's underlying rationale for establishing the competition. For example, if the purpose is to provide value to a company, showcase the research and analytical skills of candidates, or simulate "real life," then you will have more liberal rules on SMEs. Conversely, where the competition is more concerned with a level playing field, and assessing students' skills independent of experts, you will find more conservative rules. Bottom line, follow the rules – nothing is gained from skirting the edge and gaining an unfair advantage, whether real or perceived.

Rubric

Rubrics are the standardized set of expectations governing how teams are evaluated. The extent to which a competition employs rubrics and how judges actually use a rubric can vary widely. A good rule of thumb is that if the subject company is fictional, the competition rubric is more likely to be followed because the judges are not attached to the company and will require substantial guidance.

On the other hand, when you have company executives who have proposed a specific problem and want a solution to that problem, they are far more likely to pick the team they like most, perhaps disregarding the rubric altogether. It can be frustrating, but it is the nature of these competitions – and real life – that the metrics of evaluation are highly subjective.

Niche Competitions

We call these niche competitions because they focus on a relatively narrow element of business: industry, function, or demographics. The rules are a little different with these competitions, and success results from effectively weaving together what the rubric expects and what business strategy theory tells you to do.

These can be great learning opportunities because reality is often more complex and ambiguous than pure science can explain. There is an entire field of behavioral economics devoted to explaining the phenomena of individuals making decisions outside what traditional economics can explain. The competitions can also be frustrating because of the inherent complexity and ambiguity of the problem. You can choose to be annoyed, but we counter that the appropriate response should be "challenge accepted!" The world is full of snarly, messy, confusing problems where possible solutions seem to be contradictory. The best teams are those who incorporate and fuse business solutions together to solve a problem. The losers attempt to just "bolt on" a solution that checks a box on the rubric.

A good example is the "ethics" case competition. You may encounter a scenario in which the judges are executives from the subject company. These individuals are very concerned with the ROI of any strategy. If the team spent too much time discussing ethical implications but didn't underscore ROI for the company or how the plan fit into the company's overall strategy, the team will be evaluated poorly.

Another example is a sustainability competition with a fictional company. One of our teams focused more on ROI than sustainability and was penalized in the scoring. The lesson here is that the goal for any team should be to emphasize a solid business strategy that has a relevant return AND seamlessly incorporates niche elements of the competition. Therefore, in preparation, study different strategies employed by a variety of firms, functions, and industries related to the niche competition. What are core elements of successful strategies of companies that have "won" at ethics or sustainability? This will give you a framework you can use in your analysis and solution.

Q&A with Judges

Some competitions will give you an opportunity to have a Q&A session with the judges after the case question has been released. These help refine your solution and prevent you from spending too much time on a strategy that will be a non-starter for the company. The key for effectively preparing for this session is to ensure you are spending time researching the company and pressure-testing some ideas through advance research. We will cover this in more detail in Chapter 16.

Setting Up Your Workspace or Team Room

Most hosts will provide you workspace to use during the competition. You'll likely be spending some serious quality time in this room, so make sure you set up a good space in which to work.

If possible, determine in advance which resources the team rooms will have available so you know how and what to prepare. For example, will it have a team screen you can plug into? Does the room have whiteboards? If not, do you need to budget to purchase large newsprint when you arrive? It is also important to remember that you are guests of the host institution; make sure you follow the rules set by the host regarding use of the space. It is a huge undertaking to host these competitions and an honor and privilege to be included. Respect that at all times.

Don't overlook the human aspects of the team room by just focusing on technology and supplies. Think about drinks and snacks (these may or may not be provided by the competition) and bringing warm clothing as classroom buildings are notoriously cold. You're going to be pushing yourselves very hard and must ensure you're in good shape, physically and mentally.

Schedule (24-Hour versus Other Formats)

The balance of time varies based on the structure of the competition. Remember that the 24-hour format is both a blessing and a curse. You know that no matter what, the competition has limited time in which you can work the case. Our successful teams get little or no sleep during these competitions.

Our motto of "Sleep When You Win" is not an exaggeration. That means these competitions can be very physically demanding. Knowledge is power – you will know this is coming and can prepare for it. Make sure to spend the week before getting as much sleep as possible and eating healthy foods. This will make your all-nighter easier to manage.

Additionally, this type of format is known to put a strain on the team. The stress and lack of sleep can combine to spark conflict among the most agreeable teammates. Prepare for this in advance – discuss how you react to lack of sleep, agree on how the team plans to use its time, and consider how you will manage the inevitable conflict. Preparing for this in advance will neutralize most issues that arise during 24-hour case competitions.

It is likely that most of you will face a work all-nighter at some point, particularly if you are going into consulting or investment banking. This is good training for that situation, and you will be amazed at what you can produce during a short period.

Exercise to Prepare for a 24-hour Case

The best way to train for a 24-hour case competition is to precisely simulate the structure. When preparing our teams for a 24-hour case, we expect them to complete one 24-hour case in advance. There are a lot of creative ways to work this into your training schedule. The most effective is an actual 24-hour case in which you give the team the case problem on a Friday morning, for example, and then have a team of judges evaluate the team's performance on a Saturday morning.

An alternative is to provide the case to the students at 7 a.m. on a Saturday and require the slide deck to be turned in on Sunday morning, but the staff or faculty evaluate it on Monday (which limits weekend commitments). You can also use the honor system and tell the students they are allowed to work on the case for only 24 hours. The most important element is proving to the students what they can accomplish in 24 hours and to pressure-test the team to see where their process needs work. The exercises in which they get little or no sleep are particularly valuable because students will then know what to expect from the real thing.

"Practice does not make perfect. Only perfect practice makes perfect." (Often credited to the legendary football coach Vince Lombardi.) We've provided you a wealth of tips and tricks to maximize the value of your preparation for the competition. Employ these suggestions and you will be well on your way to perfect practice.

CHAPTER 15: SUBJECT MATTER EXPERTS

Searching the web for relevant research is helpful, but your results are limited in that everything you will find has already been written without your specific situation in mind. Contacting an expert, though, gives you the chance to ask very targeted questions to home in on exactly the information you need to direct and defend your recommendations. If you have the time and permission to do so, you should make an effort to talk to several experts in areas related to the case.

The rules for contacting individuals outside of your team vary widely from competition to competition, ranging from absolutely zero contact to total free license to contact anyone you want for background on the situation, company, or industry. Obviously, you must conform strictly to these rules, and if there is any ambiguity about whether contacting a particular person is allowed, you should ask the competition coordinators. If that isn't possible, play it safe and avoid any appearance of impropriety, which could risk disqualification. The rest of this section applies to situations in which contacting external experts is permitted.

Who Are the Experts We Want?

Consultants: Management or strategy consultants can be a valuable source of knowledge because they've essentially done what you're being asked to do – come into a particular situation from the outside, diagnose a problem, and design or implement a solution. Ideally, find someone who has been in the consulting world for a little while (a partner is better than someone only six months out of an MBA program); a partner will be more likely to have served multiple clients in the same industry or functional vertical and can offer a broader perspective.

Getting time with consultants can be challenging, though, as most of the big firms pull long hours (60-80 hours per week on average), and many require considerable travel.

Faculty: Many faculty members have served as outside consultants to industry in addition to (usually) conducting their own research projects for academic publications. It's also not uncommon, particularly in business schools, to find faculty who have been practitioners during their careers. They're also usually a great source of additional contacts from the large numbers of students who have passed through their classes over the years and are now distributed in numerous organizations.

Employees or Former Employees: Unsurprisingly, current and former employees can be a great source of information. However, you should carefully scrutinize the role(s) a particular contact has held within an organization, ensuring that this employee has sufficient visibility and experience to advise you.

For example, you may have a best friend who works as a salesperson for John Deere in California. If the case is related to bringing a new agricultural product line to the company's North American customers, it could be a valuable conversation. However, if Deere is trying to learn how it can better serve customers with limited access to water in West Africa, you might look for a better expert (your friend might be able to help you find another contact).

Also do not discount the value in conducting site visits to talk to frontline employees if the case is relevant. For example, one of our teams was competing in a national case sponsored by a large restaurant chain that had several locations in our area. Team members visited one of the locations, told the manager about the competition, and were given a full tour, an interview with the manager, and the opportunity to observe daily operations. This experience was invaluable in helping the team develop a solution – and they won the case competition.

Customers: A firm's customers can offer excellent insights into pricing, competitive advantage (i.e., why the customer picked this firm over competitors), the purchase process, post-sale support, and other issues. However, you should be very selective in your use of customers and take their insights in context with the case.

For example, it's particularly tempting to use family and friends for B2C cases because they're easily accessible – your parents may be lifelong Tide detergent customers – but you probably don't want to base strategic recommendations on a sample size of one household. However, an alumnus of your school who is the CIO of a major airline that purchases IBM technology to manage its scheduling system could be an ideal contact for a case about new B2B applications of the firm's Watson artificial intelligence platform.

Partners and Suppliers: Channel partners or suppliers to a particular company can provide a valuable perspective. Contacting a vendor is just about a must for any supply-chain-related case, as would be a retailer for any sales/marketing case that involves a CPG firm. For example, a P&G case about rationalizing its brand portfolio would be a great reason to contact a buyer or merchandiser at Walmart.

Competitors: This one can be a little riskier. Competitors can certainly supply a valuable outside perspective, but you have to be very careful how you present any information you receive from them; executives can be very sensitive about competitors' involvement. First, you'll often find a "they're the enemy" mindset in place, and the judges may resent your contacting a competitor. Tying into that mindset, the judges may take a negative stance on any strategy rooted in what a competitor might be doing or thinking. No one wants to be seen as a copycat. Any time you say "We talked with your main competitor, and they said ... " you're putting yourself at risk of backlash. Even if you try not to name the company, they may push you on it, making the whole situation even more awkward. They might be fine with it ... but they might not.

Competitors are therefore best used in the early phases to help anonymously validate or disprove a direction instead of being cited specifically as the driver. If they do give you a great nugget of information, try to find another reputable but less controversial source to support the same idea.

How and When Do We Use Experts?

There are two primary categories we've found in which an expert can be useful.

1. Setting the direction
2. Supporting specific components

Setting the Direction

Early in the case you may find yourself with an array of options you can pursue to address a challenge. Consulting with experts can be an excellent option to validate or eliminate a particular option. Notice that we are not advocating looking to experts to provide you with a list of options. One of the quickest ways to frustrate an expert is to come to them empty-handed. You can't just start the conversation with "What should we do?" Part of being respectful of that person's time means sufficiently preparing for the conversation.

Your team must bring something to which experts can react: "We're seeing three potential directions we can go with this ... " Now the expert has a starting point and can more effectively guide you. Experts can frequently suggest an approach you may not have even considered, and even if your team's ideas are quickly thrown out, you'll often find that you will get a much better result if you started with something rather than nothing.

These early conversations are quite useful in uncovering "fatal flaws" that may be more nuanced. For example, an expert may have actually tried the approach you're suggesting and found that it was impractical because regulatory requirements made it cost-prohibitive. It is MUCH better to pressure-test ideas early, uncovering flaws, than to find them within a few hours of the deadline ... or worse, during Q&A when a judge asks, "Did you know about the FCC regulations that essentially prohibit what you're recommending?"

Remember, you want to document these option-eliminating conversations in the Appendix (if not the main deck), because it details how your team evaluated different paths and how you ultimately chose the direction you did.

Experienced strategy consultants are particularly useful at this phase because they frequently have to come into a situation with little background, diagnose the problem, and develop a turnaround plan. A seasoned consultant will know where the big problems typically occur and may have attempted several different fixes along the way.

Faculty are also helpful here as they may have conducted research on multiple companies and/or served as consultants themselves.

Supporting Specific Components

Once your team has settled on a strategy to tackle the problem, experts can help you add detail to your recommendations and enhance your implementation plan. For example, let's say you are suggesting an acquisition strategy for a regional bank that wants to expand its footprint. An M&A expert in this space can tell you which factors you should consider in an acquisition target and how you can calculate a valuation, while a human capital or HR expert can tell you which steps are needed to successfully integrate two separate cultures or organizational structures.

Finding and Contacting Experts

This is all about unleashing the power of your network, particularly second-degree connections – you know someone who knows someone who is an expert. The name of the game is to quickly identify a list of experts, prioritize your outreach, and arrange a 20- or 30-minute call.

The approach you take will depend on the structure and rules of the competition. If permissible, delegating this task to coaches can enable the team to spend its time elsewhere. This is particularly helpful in a 24-hour structure in which time is extremely limited. If coaches are not allowed to assist, the team will have to manage the outreach on its own.

Where to Look

Your best tool for finding contacts is LinkedIn – as of the publication date of this book, there is no other platform that can readily connect you to other professionals and enable you to search for contacts with specific backgrounds (e.g., alumni from your school now working for Ford). If you don't already have a solid LinkedIn profile and haven't made the effort to connect with classmates, faculty, former colleagues, visiting speakers, or alumni you've met, then start on this immediately. Alumni databases can be useful, but our experience has been that LinkedIn is typically more up-to-date.

Faculty and staff at your MBA program can also be quite helpful as they'll be able to draw upon interactions with former students who have left to become successful alumni across a wide spectrum of industries and functions.

Advance Notification

Start looking through your network well before the competition starts. If you know the company or topic, or if you have a long time in which to complete the case, the contact process is easy.

A 24-hour structure, though, in which you don't know the case and/or company in advance, requires more planning and teamwork. Once the competition kicks off, you're going to have a VERY narrow window in which to find, secure the cooperation of, and speak with your experts. Check the rules first, then use these suggestions to prepare.

Notify faculty, staff, and fellow students: Before you leave for the competition, send an email to stakeholders from your school to let them know that you're participating in a case competition and that you are allowed to consult outside experts. These stakeholders might include:

- Faculty
- Career Services staff (have lots of company contacts)
- Development and Alumni staff (often have a very strong contact list)
- Deans and Program Directors
- Other students – club presidents (e.g., Consulting, Finance) can be particularly helpful

Ask whether they would be okay with helping you secure experts on a very tight timeline for the competition.

The idea is that as soon as you know the topic of the case, you send the details to your support team so they can start helping you line up contacts immediately.

To make it easier on them, we've found it's a good idea to give them an email template that they can customize for outreach rather than expecting them to start from scratch. Here's an example of what they might send out:

> *Dear X,*
>
> *I'm emailing you because a student team from State University is competing in the Multilateral Ethics Case Competition this weekend in San Diego (details below), and they may need 20-30 minutes of your time later today for a phone conversation. The topic is (insert topic here), and teams are allowed to contact outside experts. Given your experience in (insert background here), I think you could be a great resource.*
>
> *Their time window is very tight, so the conversation will have to be sometime between 10 a.m. and 2 p.m. today. If you would be willing to assist, could you reply to this note with your available times and preferred phone number?*
>
> *Our team is facing off against 15 other programs including Tech, Southwestern, and Ivy, and they have just 24 hours to formulate a recommendation and develop a presentation. They'll present to a panel of executive judges Saturday morning and then conduct a Q&A session.*
>
> *This is an excellent learning opportunity for the students and a chance to win $10K, and winning would further strengthen State's brand.*
>
> *We would all appreciate any time that you could offer. Also please keep in mind that because they're under a very tight deadline, they likely won't have time to contact more than just a couple of individuals, and we're doing our best to line*

*up as many as we can. Depending on the direction they plan
to take, it is possible that they might not contact you.*

Please let me know if you have any questions.
Thanks,
X

Once you know the case topic, all you have to do is email it to your
support team; they can add the details to the template and send
the emails to experts.

Note: The portion of the note at the end that indicates the expert
might not be contacted is VITAL to avoid any ruffled feathers if a
team doesn't call. Trust us on this.

We'd recommend you designate one team member responsible for
managing the scheduling of calls. As your experts reply, the follow-
up email can be something like this:

*Thanks so much, John! I am cc'ing (team member name)
from the State team on this note, so she can coordinate next
steps if the team is able to connect with you.*

Hi Team Member Name,

*John Doe (LinkedIn) is a State alum and Engagement
Manager with McKinsey who has substantial experience in
the insurance industry, particularly in helping firms develop
digital marketing strategies. He has offered to chat with
you (see availability below) if your team thinks his
experience aligns with the direction you plan to take for the
competition.*

Thanks,
X

Best practice here is for the support team member to include a link to the expert's LinkedIn profile so the team can use that background to help determine whether the conversation would be a good use of time.

Notifying your own network: you may not know all the details about the case problem until the kickoff of the 24-hour session, but you may know the broad topic (e.g., ethics, sustainability, human capital) or even the company name in advance. If this is the case, then you can start lining up experts yourself using an email structure similar to the above.

Pre-call Preparation

Once you've locked in time with an expert, make sure the team is ready to have a productive conversation so that A) you can get actionable information that will support your case and B) you make a good impression with the expert. You'll obviously have less time to prepare for a 24-hour case than you will for other formats, but there are a few quick steps you can still take to prepare.

- **LinkedIn Review** – assuming the expert has a profile, have the team review it to get a good sense of background.

- **Web Search** – check to see if this person has written any blogs or articles related to your topic. It's not uncommon for faculty and senior consultants to have published works.

- **Potential Directions and Questions** – you cannot come into the conversation completely empty-handed. You'll need a hypothesis about the problem that your experts can react to, otherwise they are likely to become frustrated or be unable to give you useful information in the limited time allotted. If time permits, you can email them some questions in advance so they can come into the call with prepared thoughts.

The physical preparations should not be overlooked either. Make sure you have a quiet place to take the call and a reliable phone or video conference tool so you can clearly hear and see the person. If you are going to use a video conference tool (e.g., Skype, Hangouts, Facetime), make sure you're dressed presentably and the location you use for the call is uncluttered and professional-looking.

Managing the Call

You might be a little nervous making these calls, which is totally normal. However, YOU need to take the lead rather than relying on the expert to do so. You should have a plan to get the conversation going. The conversation may not go in the direction you planned, but a structured kickoff will get the ideas moving more quickly and in a more focused manner. And it will make a MUCH better impression on your expert.

Once you get the expert on the phone, there are a few things that will help the conversation progress smoothly. Here are the basic steps the call should take:

Introductions: ideally the team member who coordinated the call should start things off. Begin by thanking the expert for the time and assistance and then briefly naming the people in the room. There's no need to waste time on individual introductions:

> *This is Jason, and I have my team members Marc and Kara in the room. First off, we want to thank you for taking the time to chat with us.*

Brief Status Overview: tell the expert where you are in your research and why you want to talk to them.

We just received the case this morning, and it's focused on expanding ABC Furniture's online sales. Based on the overview from their CMO, customer experience is their top differentiator, and they're worried about losing their edge with online sales.

We're so far considering options including mobile devices for in-store sales personnel, webcams on the showroom floor, pricing discounts for online purchases, and a virtual room-designer. We understand that you've done a lot of work in creating omni-channel strategies for retailers and would like to learn more about the components you think are critical to success.

By doing this, you've explained the basic problem, highlighted a few early ideas, and shown the expert that you have considered where she can add value.

Confirm comfort with approach: Explain your plan for the call and ask if the expert agrees or has a better suggestion.

We've pulled together a list of questions for you and can walk through them one at a time, or if you have some initial thoughts you'd like to cover first, we can start there. Do you have a preference?

Gather information: the insights or advice should start flowing at this point. Other team members should be able to jump in with questions or comments, identifying themselves in turn:

This is Kara, could you expand upon how and why you segmented online customers differently from traditional customers?

Obviously, you should be taking notes on what is said, and not just on the content – look for direct quotes when possible.

Asking for resources: if the expert is quoting studies, articles, or other sources, ask whether you can get an emailed link or attachments. These can be excellent sources to shape your strategy, references to cite in the main deck or Appendix.

Closing out: as you wrap up your list of questions, you should ask the following:

- *Are there any other questions we should have asked or factors we should consider when building our recommendation?*

- *Are there any other articles or materials you think we should review?*

- *If time permits – Are there any other experts you think it would be beneficial for us to interview? (If yes, ask if they can introduce you.)*

- *Would it be all right if we cited you as a source in our recommendations? If you don't want us to use your name, would it be okay if we used an approximate title and company name?*

Then thank the person again for the time and mention that you'll provide an update on how things turned out.

Following the Call

You definitely want to send a thank-you email to every expert with whom you spoke as well as any members of your support team (e.g., faculty, program staff), and an actual handwritten note in the mail is so unusual now as to be really *memorable*. If an expert's insights materially contributed to your recommendations, tell them how helpful they were.

If there is a press release by your school or the competition host that provides details on the event, you can send that link as well. It will reflect positively on you and the program if you do (and negatively if you don't), so do NOT overlook this step.

Learning to leverage outside resources will serve you very well throughout your career. It's foolish not to look outside one's own base of knowledge to tackle an unknown problem, and learning how to identify, secure, and apply expertise from others is a key component to professional development.

Chapter 16: Q&A with Judges

Some competitions will provide time to conference call with or meet face-to-face with judges, either as a group or as individual teams. Take advantage of this opportunity!

We once participated in a competition at which the teams were given the contact information for the head judge and told that they could call within a certain block of time. Our team was the only one of six that took advantage of this. The competition organizer was utterly flabbergasted – as were we! If you are offered such an opportunity, do not pass it up; these individuals will be able to give you insights that almost no one else will. Meetings in which your team visits alone with the judges are ideal because other teams won't get a sense of the direction your team is headed, but group settings can still provide considerable information and insight. Some things to keep in mind:

- Make sure your questions are those that cannot be found elsewhere. Keep in mind that these judges may remember you when you are actually competing, and you don't want to be the team that asks the question that shows up in basic research.
- The alternative also holds true. If you ask thoughtful and insightful questions, judges may remember you positively during the competition.
- Be respectful of all participants during this process. In the large group setting, it is important to show good sportsmanship. Go into this as a professional and stay that way. This is not the time to act superior or arrogant. Gather and assimilate all the information you can. If you don't think much of another team's direction or questions, this is the time to keep your game face on.

This chapter is brief, but it is quite important. Taking advantage of these offered Q&A sessions with the judges is usually pivotal in the research and analysis process. Don't pass up this opportunity!

CHAPTER 17: MANAGING TEAM TIME

Preparation time

Generally speaking, three to four weeks of preparation time before a competition is sufficient. At this point you will have the tools of successful case work in your box, and now it is all about deploying skills for the case. You will sometimes know the industry and even the case company before the competition. If you do, the key components of preparation are:

- Conduct company/industry research
- Identifying SMEs
- Contacting SMEs
- Developing approach, strategy, and story
- Delivering first practice run and receiving feedback
- Completing the final practice run

Depending on how much time you have, these elements can be scaled for a longer or shorter time, but the components stay the same. How much you know about the nature of the case will determine the content and structure of practice cases and may change the number of or backgrounds of your SMEs.

Building In Time for Practice Cases

Running practice cases is vital to building team competency, and we recommend using two types: 1. A broad strategy case and 2. A more narrow, targeted case. Bottom line, the most important elements are to research the case or industry, learn as much as you can about both, and then practice running through cases at least twice. Four weeks is an ideal schedule, but this can be scaled down to two weeks if necessary.

The above discussion should cover what you need for most competitions. You may encounter "blind" competitions in which you know neither the industry nor the company (and/or problem) in advance. In that situation, SMEs aren't really an option, and three to four weeks is still enough time to conduct at least two practice cases.

If you know the case in advance, you will be working on the actual company and problem. Alternatively, if you know just the company or industry, you should create practice cases to closely simulate the anticipated case as best you can. In other words, it's your best guess. These practice cases will allow you to simulate one broad strategy case and one more specific or targeted case.

Additionally, at least one of these two practices should simulate the structure of the competition. For example, if you will participate in a 24-hour case competition, one of your practices should be limited to a 24-hour period. Building confidence with the format will give you an advantage over other teams who have not worked with that format before.

Pitfalls

Failing to spend enough time practicing the presentation and Q&A is the most common pitfall we see when teams are preparing their cases. Note the graphic above – teams will routinely spend only a small percentage of their time practicing their presentation or the Q&A portion of the presentation. At least 20 percent of the time should be spent on practice. That means that in a 24-hour case, about 5 hours should be devoted to refining the story, practicing the presentation, and anticipating questions and preparing responses. Too often, we've seen teams leave the presentation slides or storyline until the last couple of hours. Consequently, the story is disjointed and the presenters unprepared.

Time management during the event:

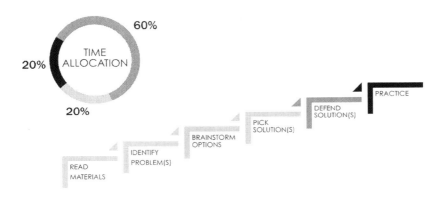

TIME ALLOCATION

60%

20%

20%

READ MATERIALS

IDENTIFY PROBLEM(S)

BRAINSTORM OPTIONS

PICK SOLUTION(S)

DEFEND SOLUTION(S)

PRACTICE

Timeline: Building the Case

A poor effort in presentation will generally lead the evaluator to perceive the team poorly. It doesn't matter how strong your idea or analysis is – if you cannot effectively communicate that idea, it won't matter. Just like making errors on your résumé, it is a sloppy representation. Even if the judges are fully aware of how or why they are evaluating you, they will score you poorly if the presentation isn't polished and your story isn't concise and tightly written.

Conflict Management:

A healthy tension within the team can be a valuable asset. You should be pushing one another and pressure-testing ideas. This is a good thing – *a team that agrees on everything is usually missing something*. Constructive feedback is respectful of the other person and specific to the task at hand.

A useful approach is to determine ahead of time how the team will make decisions. Are you going to go with the majority or do you want consensus? Pick a plan, stick to it, and be prepared to get on board. During competitions in which there is a short turnaround time, you should go with majority rules. When planning your time strategy, identify a time when you will brainstorm and set a deadline for committing to a plan of action – and then stick to it. It is often useful to identify someone on the team who serves as the timekeeper.

These competitions can be stressful, and where stress exists, so do short tempers, particularly when there is a short deadline. Understanding and expecting this is a huge advantage and is the reason we recommend practice cases that simulate the real environment. Once you have an idea of how each person responds to stressful situations, you can all work together in the middle of the high-pressure competition.

This approach will go a long way toward avoiding conflict in the heat of the competition. And, avoiding conflict is really the best way to manage conflict. That isn't to say that you shouldn't challenge one another and provide constructive feedback, it is just that these suggestions will help avoid unproductive conflict.

If you find yourself in the middle of intense conflict, take a break and walk away for 15 or so minutes. Have each person walk away and do what they need to do to relieve tension. That may be taking a walk and getting fresh air, listening to music and dancing around, or doing some pushups or yoga. Doesn't matter what it is, but take a pause and blow off the steam – *just disengage*. When you come back, take a moment and focus back on the goal. Re-engage your prefrontal cortex in place of the more emotion-driven part of your brain. These steps will alleviate major contributors to unhealthy conflict and get you back on the right path.

Practice Runs

Plan at least two or three full practice runs of the presentation before you actually deliver it. Clock each person's split time so you can get a feel for whether you are ahead of, on, or behind pace as you transition between presenters. Though your closer has the ultimate responsibility for wrapping up within the allotted time, everyone preceding the closer should be monitoring their own delivery to ensure adequate time is left at the end. You CANNOT run over your time!

Appendix Review

In addition to practice runs of the main presentation, you should take time before the competition to review the Appendix slides. Include this in the time you budget for practice. The entire team should be familiar with the Appendix so each person is aware of what is at their disposal for the Q&A with the judges. This will also take place during the halftime check – but you do not want to wait for that. Make sure that about 10 percent of your practice time is budgeted for a review of the assets in your Appendix.

Build a plan incorporating the recommendations above. It is tempting to jump into the competition, but establishing a clear working timeline will ensure you are spending your time where it is most valuable and not skipping over important elements of success.

Chapter 18: Checklist

Remember the importance of form as well as function. If your deck is sloppy, executives will assume your analysis is sloppy. They'll push hard on your numbers and rationale. If your deck is clean and consistent, well edited, and detail-checked, it shows that you are business-oriented and professional.

During our consulting and corporate days, we spent time with teams going through every slide of a deck before presentation to executives. The eyes of three or more people were focused on the screen to catch every little error within a slide and across the entire deck (up to 100 slides). It was time-intensive, but it usually resulted in catching items that would have undermined the team's credibility. The more you do this, the better you will get, and soon you'll be the one picking apart a deck and pointing out that the second textbox is one or two pixels to the left, or you've misused apostrophes, or you've used "you're" instead of "your."

Here is a checklist you should give every member of the team to review before the competition begins. We'd also recommend printing a copy and posting it somewhere in the team room.

If you're in a 24-hour case, the Slide Master should review it at least two hours before the deck submission deadline. We recommend scheduling time right before the deadline for the entire team to review the deck with this list.

SLIDE-LEVEL CHECK

Use this checklist on every slide in the main deck (and Appendix if possible)

Editing and formatting
- Professional font – best if matches company's standard
- Same type style used throughout
- Same case used throughout
- Nothing smaller than 14-point (except footnotes or cited sources)
- Layout and styles consistent (e.g., all headings same)
- Bulleted or numbered lists are consistent and professional
- Bold or italic text used sparingly – avoid underlined text
- Consistent use of text and image alignment
- Correct punctuation, grammar, spelling
- Limited (if any) use of idiomatic speech, clichés, jargon, or slang

Colors and Display
- Same colors used throughout – best if matches company's standard
- Color differences are intentional for emphasis or organization
- Adequate contrast between text and backgrounds, (e.g. no gray on gray)
- Review slides on actual screen if possible

Objects (Textboxes, Arrows)
- Style is consistent (e.g., all rounded corners or all square corners)
- Spacing consistent between items
- Same size unless scale is used purposely to highlight differences

- Objects are aligned correctly (vertical or horizontal)
- Borders match
- Shadows on or off (off is better)
- Corresponding text is aligned consistently (left, right, centered, justified)
- No text overlapping object borders
- Connectors either in contact or identical distance apart
- Icons are purposeful, professional, and not copyrighted or watermarked

Images
- Not blurry or pixelated when displayed on a large screen
- Borders are consistent
- No watermarks or copyrighted work
- Corporate logos are current and match EXACTLY
- Align with story
- Professional and appropriate for audience (0% doubt)

Data, Graphs and Tables
- Font matches rest of deck and is legible
- Units of measure labeled
- Scaling appropriate (e.g., $250M and not $250,000,000.00)
- Consistent use of decimal points and commas
- Axes labeled
- Labels and colors easily discernable
- Borders consistent
- Colors and styles consistent

Animation
- Every animation has a purpose (and justification)
- Test thoroughly on large screen in presentation mode
- No timing delay over 1 second unless absolutely required

- Simple entrances and exits (e.g., Appear or Fade) - no flying or bouncing

Appendix
- Links are all active and correct - double-check this
- Navigation page contains links to main deck slides and Appendix slides

Other
- Spelling - double-checked
- Sources - cited on page
- Acronyms make sense or are explained on first usage
- Page numbers - conform to rules or corporate standards

DECK-LEVEL CHECK

Compare slides throughout entire deck for consistency

All items above, PLUS:

- Page number location, style
- Tracker (optional bar at top or bottom to track progress)
- Animation style consistent
- Same icons or pictures for consistently referenced items or topics
- Terminology consistent (e.g., customers or clients or users)
- Units of measure the same throughout ($M versus $MM) - use company's standard (look in the Annual Report or 10K)
- Team anonymity
- No school colors
- No geographic references

HANDOUT CHECK

- Preview deck in color AND b&w to ensure all text and objects are visible
- Restructure or remove any animation-related or static objects that overlap
- Page numbers are visible and in order

PRESENTER CHECK

- All school-related identifiers removed from clothing, bags, laptops, etc.
- Everyone has reviewed main deck and Appendix to know what is available
- Conduct at least two full dry-runs for timing
- Clothing and accessories are appropriate type and fit
- Clothing is cleaned, polished, organized, professional
- Meticulous grooming

This is by no means an exhaustive list, and you may well add some of your own items. However, you should get in the habit of a structured verification process any time you are presenting to an audience. Stress is high and time is short, which makes for a mistake-prone environment. Process is your ally!

Chapter 19: Presentation Structure and Styles

Introductions and Exits

The competition begins the minute your team enters the competition room. You should walk into the room in character, and carry it through until you walk back out. When you enter the room, you may be asked to load your presentation, or it may be already pre-loaded.

Once the presentation is set to go, your team should approach the judges to shake their hands and make eye contact. Smile, put your shoulders back, look them in the eye, and give them a firm (not bone-crushing and not too soft) handshake while you introduce yourself to each judge. At the close of the presentation and Q&A period, you will do the same: approach the judges, shake their hands, and thank them. Then leave – calmly, confidently, and professionally.

Opening and Closing

Your opening is the first impression the judges will have of your team. When deciding which team member will deliver the opening, it is important that you select one of your best and most engaging presenters. This person will set the tone for the presentation and is responsible for "hooking" the audience. We've heard judges say more than once that a presentation can be won or lost in the first 5 minutes.

Similarly, your closer needs to be another of your strongest presenters. This person must pull together the entire presentation and "close the deal" with the judges. This presenter should pay attention to how the judges are receiving each element of the presentation, so they understand which points to reinforce and which may need clarification. Additionally, this person must condense or stretch time as necessary depending on how the rest of the team manages time. Without question, assignment of these roles is critical. It can be the same person, or two different people – but the delivery must be outstanding.

Presenter Transitions

Each person on the team should use about the same time during the presentation. This is flexible, because the transitions should make sense, but the judges should perceive that time is balanced among the team. The flow of the story should drive how the presentation is distributed, rather than the distribution of presenters driving the story flow. You'll choose which person is best to deliver each section, but be prepared to shift things a bit if the story flow demands it.

When handing off the presentation from one person to another, each person involved has a role. Here is a well-received sequence:

1. Presenter A: Now that we've discussed X, here is Presenter B (say the person's first name) to discuss Y ...
2. Presenter A then moves to the rear of the presenting area and Presenter B moves to the front ...
3. Presenter B: Thanks Presenter A (say the person's first name), now we're going to discuss Y.

This structure provides a smooth transition by introducing both the new topic and the new presenter. It also helps ensure continuity within the presentation and keeps the judges on track as you move from one person to another.

An additional element is to be mindful of is the number of transitions during the presentation. Generally speaking, you want each presenter to speak only once. The only exception is if you have the same person open and close the presentation. Adding more transitions uses time and wastes precious content delivery time handing off. Avoid that by keeping transitions to a minimum.

Avoiding Gimmicks and Clichés

We once held a tryout for a case competition in which the subject company was an agricultural firm that grew, harvested, and sold oranges. To open the case, the leadoff presenter tossed an orange up and down while delivering his opening. Attention grabbing? Yes. What a judging panel will respond positively to? No.

The point of business case competitions is to simulate the real world. In the realm of business, we do not use gimmicks or tricks to grab attention. It is perceived as unprofessional, and even if it attracts attention, it is the wrong kind and won't result in a win.

The other tactic we've seen (which we've never seen used successfully) is the dramatic quote or story at the beginning of the presentation. "One hundred years ago, Mr. Jones opened a small factory in Smallville. He was a self-made man who worked tirelessly to create the most amazing business empire."

Or starting with a slide containing only a quote:

"To crush your enemies and see them driven before you is the greatest thing in life." ˜ Mother Theresa (or was that Conan?)

As with other gimmicks, this is usually seen for what it is – gratuitous dramatic flair. The judges have no time for nonsense. They will perceive this as your creating "fillers" because you don't have enough content. Don't let your audience think your presentation is fluffy – and that's what they'll think if you try such gimmicks.

Attention to stylistic details can be the determining factor between first and second place. You will be competing with other teams who are smart, have invested time, and are well prepared. Spend the time to make sure that each nuance of your presentation is strong and ties together smoothly and concisely.

CHAPTER 20: Q&A STYLE AND TECHNIQUES

Competitions are often won or lost during the Q&A. A lot of teams can perform well during the presentation portion of the competition, but only the best teams master the art of Q&A. As part of our team preparation process, we put just as much emphasis on Q&A as we do on the main presentation. We'll cover a few stylistic elements that will help ensure Q&A success.

The Q&A is the opportunity for the judges to resolve questions and issues they have with your pitch. Most teams view Q&A as simply answering questions, but it is so much more than that. It is also your chance to showcase elements of your strategy that would not fit into the presentation, and to make sure the judges see the depth of your research. The team can also show the judges the breadth and depth of its team members. Judges will often select winners based the perceived strength of the overall team. Q&A is the best chance to display this knowledge because most judges know that anyone can memorize a speech, but the Q&A can't be scripted.

Balance Among Team Members

Each person on the team should be able to discuss the strategy. If one or two individuals dominate Q&A then you create two equally negative impressions. First, the people not answering questions are seen as weak team members who are not equal contributors. Second, the dominating individuals are jerks or the team is dysfunctional.

Each person on the team should be prepared to answer questions, and there should be balance among the team in terms of the number of questions answered. This creates the impression that everyone is aligned and equally strong – a winning impression.

Assigning Roles for Q&A

Each team member is usually responsible for different sections of developing and delivering the content. The team member who delivers the content is usually assigned the role of running point on Q&A. Therefore, that person should be the first person to answer a question about that section. Then other team members can join in. This makes the process more efficient than waiting to see who is ready to answer. Remember that the physical distribution of the team is important; you should position yourselves in an arc or gentle "U" shape so you can see one another and use visual cues. If the point person doesn't take the lead immediately, then another person can speak up.

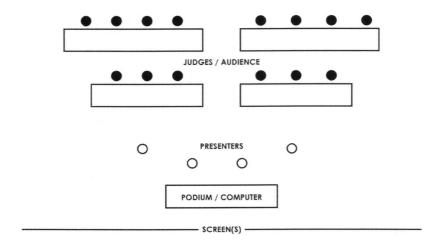

Positioning

In addition to determining who will take the lead on answering each category of question, you should determine who will run point on displaying the slide Appendix. Is there one person who was responsible for pulling together the slides and making them cohesive? Then that person is a natural fit. Alternatively, pair up for each section and have one person answer questions and the other bring up slides.

This should appear seamless to the judges. The audience should not notice the slides being brought up on the screen - it should be so well orchestrated that it seems natural. This sends a strong subliminal message to your audience that your team is operating at peak performance. Planning for this is important, because you'll be bringing up a lot of backup slides.

With the most effective teams we've seen, anyone on the team could run the Appendix. The smooth, flawless teams are aligned so that each person knows the Appendix well enough to jump in and get to the necessary slide. You still want to have point people so everyone isn't pouncing on the computer at the same time, but make sure that everyone's familiar with ALL the content of the presentation.

A Slide for Every Question, and For Every Question a Slide

During Q&A your goal should be to display a slide to accompany the answer to any question. During preparation, you should make sure there is a backup slide for every question you can think of. When that question is asked, you say, "I'm glad you asked; here is slide number x." You can not only answer the question, but also show the judges you have command of your material.

If you get a question for which you don't have a slide that matches exactly, then bring up a slide that has some relevance to the topic. You can always draw attention to something related to the topic to strengthen your argument for your strategy - besides just answering the question. This gives you an additional opportunity to show the depth of your analysis. Whether it is senior executives or clients, this tactic is highly useful and therefore a skill worth developing.

Length of Answers

The time you spend answering questions is critically important. You want the opportunity to display as much knowledge as possible, therefore you must answer questions succinctly. This may seem counterintuitive, but the goal is to allow the judges to ask as many questions as possible, so be efficient with the time. An individual's answer to a question should last about one minute. Make sure you answer the question fully, but don't expand too much and risk that the judges don't get all their questions answered.

Are there exceptions to this? Of course! If asked how much time one should spend on an answer, we'd undoubtedly say "it depends." There are times when a team member has a great deal of information to convey, and it will take more than one minute. But try to keep your answers to under a minute as often as possible (remember most TV commercials are 30 seconds long, so a minute is a relatively long time). Adherence to succinct answers ensures that there is time for your teammates to contribute and for the judges to ask follow-up questions.

Adding Value versus Piling On

Team members need to ensure that the points they add to any answer add real value. Make sure you ask yourself whether what you are about to say actually contributes to the answer; are you speaking to add value or just to hear yourself talk?

There are a couple of cues you can pay attention to that will help. First, look at the judges. Is one of them itching to ask another question? How much time is left on the clock? If you are not sure whether your part of the answer adds value, or if a judge is obviously wanting to ask another question, or if you have only a couple of minutes left, then be quiet. Resist the urge to add on. If one or two others have already jumped in, you're probably just piling on.

Avoiding Being a Jerk

There may be an occasion in which you think the judges are asking dumb questions. You may wonder whether they were even listening to the presentation or even read the case. Sure, this is annoying and frustrating. You are tired, you have worked your bum off on the case, and THIS is the question they ask? No matter what - DO NOT IN ANY WAY BE SHORT, SARCASTIC, OR SNARKY. Regardless of what prompts your frustration, you must answer the question without the slightest hint of annoyance. If you do demonstrate frustration or annoyance, you will be perceived as a jerk - no matter what. This will kill you no matter how well the rest of the presentation went.

"A simple google search ... " and "What you've got to understand" are classic examples of phrases that make you sound like a condescending jerk. And watch your body language. Putting your hands up with palms out conveys that you are defensive or are trying to suppress the judges. Hands on your hips, or crossing your arms while responding to questions, will also convey that you disagree or find the questions contemptible.

Besides making the judges decide against your team, this also serves to cut off the dialogue between you and the judges. It creates an unnecessarily contentious environment, which makes your audience uncomfortable. Think of each question as a gift, an opportunity to further connect and better communicate your strategy. After all, if the question is not asked, you will not get to create the most clarity possible and persuade the audience that your solution is the best one.

How to Correct Mistakes on the Fly

You may hear a teammate answer a question incorrectly, or you might see a judge react negatively to an answer. Let's say you have just the point that will correct the course. *The number one most important thing to do in this situation is to not contradict your teammate.* If you do, the judges will conclude that your team is not well coordinated and aligned – which is worse than being wrong.

In improvisation, you learn the art of adding to a conversation with the phrase "Yes, and ..." This works well during Q&A. You can add on to your teammate's comment by starting with "Yes, and ... " and then provide corrected information. It is completely fine if your addition (subtly) contradicts what your team member says as long as it is positioned as an additional point.

How to Practice for Q&A

At the very least, make sure your practice cases include the Q&A portion. This is the minimum level of effort that will give the team practice at answering questions. Our most successful teams do two things very well; they anticipate questions and they find ways to highlight items in the Appendix. Great teams spend time anticipating questions that judges may ask, and they quiz one another to practice answering the questions – and to determine who takes point on certain categories of questions.

A useful strategy during practice is to have the coach or a volunteer track the number of questions each person answers. Keep track of who was the first to answer and who added on to others' answers. The target is to achieve balance, so collecting and reviewing this data during practice will illustrate how balanced your team is and show you how to achieve balance.

Great teams review all the items in their Appendix and anticipate ways these slides can be used during Q&A. For example, we were once coaching a team during the break between round one and round two and reviewed their appendices with them. The team went slide by slide through a 40-page Appendix and identified several different ways the slides could be used to respond to questions. During the final, the students not only answered the questions posed, they also brought up new points using the slides when the opportunity arose. This is possible only if you are prepared and you know your content inside and out.

It is our experience that the question and answer period is as important, if not more important, than the presentation itself. Teams can practice and deliver a solid presentation but then fall apart during the Q&A. Prepare and practice using the techniques outlined above and you will be well on your way to a win!

CHAPTER 21: HALFTIME ADJUSTMENTS

This chapter is intended for those competitions that contain multiple rounds. It's relatively common to have a competition with multiple preliminary brackets, and the winners of each bracket advance to face each other in a final round. While teams are typically not allowed to change the content of their slide deck once it is submitted, they are certainly allowed to adjust the verbal content they present.

Notice we said "adjust" and not "overhaul." You can accentuate or minimize different aspects of your strategy based on questions or feedback from the first round, but you should not completely revamp your approach between rounds.

- Your slides are frozen and need to match your verbal presentation.
- You don't want to risk breaking your time limit by overhauling what you say.
- Developing a new strategy on the fly and trying to defend it well is a recipe for disaster.

Remember a decent idea very well defended will beat a great idea with poor defense nine times out of ten.

The time between rounds varies, and it is common that teams will not know whether they advance until right before the final round. Our teams' best practice is to assume they will advance, so the preparation begins again as soon as they walk out of their first-round presentation. You can take a few minutes to walk around outside to clear your head, find some caffeine, or meditate ... but then it's back to the team room for more prep.

Note: For 24-hour cases, it may be tempting to go take a nap between rounds. Only you can really know how your body responds to long periods without sleep and whether naps are effective. We have heard students from other teams say, "I really shouldn't have taken a nap ... it really messed me up even more." We can't recall ever hearing, "That nap I took really helped ... " even once. Best practice for our teams has been to push through the whole competition and then sleep (a lot) when it's over.

Using Coaches

If permitted by the rules, this is where a coach can add a LOT of value. In many competitions, coaches will not see their team's presentation until the first round, so it is a great opportunity for you to get an outside perspective on the content and delivery of a strategy. It's also very useful to have a set of eyes in the back of the room taking in all the verbal and visual cues from the presenters and the judges. Good coaches should be taking detailed notes during the presentation on the following:

- Time split of each presenter
- Voice and body language of presenters
- Body language of judges during the presentations (e.g., judges nodded or shook their heads as a particular point was covered)
- Questions asked by judges
- Tally of which presenter fielded a question and how many times each spoke during Q&A (goal is balance across the team)
- Number and content of backup slides (main deck and Appendix) used during Q&A to defend responses; speed with which the slides were displayed
- Judges reactions or patterns in Q&A (did they focus on one area?)

Reviewing Questions

Most of the time, you're not going to get feedback from the first round until later in the day or after the competition. The only insight you'll have will be derived from the questions asked and comments made during Q&A. You should identify any themes in the questions and whether you could have addressed something more clearly in the main deck to preempt the question.

Did a judge ask you to go back into the main deck to clarify something? That's a cue. For example, you may have gotten a question like, "I'm a little confused on your segmentation slide – are you saying that we should target all eight of those new online shopper segments in addition to our current segmentation, giving us a total of 12 customer types?" You fielded the question well, explaining that you wanted to target only two of the eight segments mentioned, bringing the overall target to six segments. In the finals, then, you clarify this in the main deck with a single sentence, "So of these eight segments, we want to target only Metro Women and Affluent Students, bringing our total number of segments to six, which is in line with comparable omni-channel strategies according to Accenture."

This is also a good chance for the team and/or the coach to review who was fielding the questions. Be aware of balance and ensure that every team member is chiming in at least once and that one or two people are not dominating the entire session.

Reviewing Appendix and Main Deck

If you can use your coaches' feedback between rounds, you should walk them through your deck and the Appendix slides. We've found this to be beneficial in that the coaches can point out specific slides that can be used to address a particular question.
Your team should be in the habit of loading a backup slide (Appendix or main deck) for just about every question asked in

Q&A. Even if a coach isn't available, the team should review the deck to identify additional (or just better) slides that could be used in response to a question.

This exercise will at least familiarize the team even more with the entire deck, which you may not have had enough time for in a 24-hour case. Our experience, though, is that you will find at least one or two other slides that could have been used in Q&A.

Reviewing the Clock

If you were able to record the time splits, either through a coach or through the team members' mental notes, it's a good chance to compare times with what was rehearsed in the practice sessions. This can help you adjust your delivery a bit across presenters to either cover more content or cut back so that you're using the allotted time without pushing your deadline.

Physical Adjustments

Once you're through the presentation and Q&A, you may want to make some adjustments on your positioning. Maybe the team could not easily make eye contact with each other because of the layout of the room, and you might need to spread out a little more than planned. Or perhaps the throw angle of the projector caused one or more team members to block the screen. This is the time to make adjustments.

If you haven't already seen the room in which the final presentations will be given, try to see it as soon as possible. It's not uncommon for the final rounds to occur in an auditorium setting, while the preliminary rounds may have been in classrooms or conference rooms. You want to see the layout well before your team has to present there, so you can plan logistics and reduce the nervousness you might feel walking into a strange room to present for the first time.

Additional Practice Runs

You've got the time – use it! It's helpful to make one or two more dry runs to get comfortable with the material, integrate any changes you made, and smooth out transitions between speakers.

Coaches, this is an excellent chance for you to consult on body language, voice, eye contact, and other elements of presentation. Use the notes you took in the first round to fine-tune delivery for the finals.

Too many teams waste this opportunity by taking the time to rest or just "step away for a while." We've experienced major success by continuing to push all the way through competitions and adopting a "sleep when you win" mindset. Time is a precious asset in these competitions – don't waste a second of it!

CHAPTER 22: DEBRIEF SESSIONS

Preparing

Watch the video: An effective tool for the best feedback is watching the video recorded during practice cases. We record our teams and provide them the video as soon as possible. We expect the team to watch the video before the feedback session. This way they can develop their own impression of their performance. Students can pick out much of what needs improvement by watching their own presentation.

Mentally prepare: As you watch the video, take note of things that need to be fixed and begin to develop strategies to improve. This will put you in the proper mindset to receive feedback from others.

There is no question that it can be hard to receive tough criticism on your work. However, you will grow the most if you learn how to take and how to provide effective feedback. The model we like is based on the feedback model first outlined by the Center for Creative Leadership (CCL), which was adapted by our colleague John Walsh of the Walt Disney Co.

How to take feedback: First and foremost, consider any feedback you receive as a gift and try to not take it personally. Returning to the simile of learning to ride a bike, when you were learning, the bike (and physics) provided immediate feedback on your performance. When you fell, you weren't angry at the bike or the physical world for letting you know you needed to change something. The same should be true here.

CCL uses the acronym "RISE" in discussing how to receive feedback:

Reflect on the feedback. If you respond negatively to the feedback, you may need some extra time to reflect.

Inquire to get more information. Ask the individuals providing feedback to give more details if you need to better understand what is and is not working.

Strategize to use the feedback for better action next time. Discuss with your teammates and coaches which performance behaviors will work better.

Engage in action to do it differently. Work with your teammates to determine how you can incorporate and practice the new tactic, get more feedback, and ensure improved performance.

How to give feedback: Credible, Consistent, Concise, and Caring are the 4 C's of giving feedback. Giving feedback to others can be nerve wracking, usually because we are worried about hurting their feelings and making them angry with us. However, in a case competition, it is an incredibly powerful tool for improved performance. Providing feedback from the position of the 4 C's and using the following "SAID" model will yield considerable benefits.

Situation: Describe the situation to the person – this is why we record the presentations, because it takes the guesswork out of describing the situation; individuals can see the situation versus your trying to describe it.

Action: What is it that you observed that you want to correct or discuss for performance improvement? A video is useful here because you aren't relying on recall. You can use the rubric provided below.

Impact: Articulate what the impact of this action is on the desired outcome. You can discuss how you received the message. As a coach you may also point out how you have seen judges respond to similar behaviors in the past.

Do: What can be done in future performances to achieve a better result? In providing feedback, it is useful to be solution-oriented and provide the individual or team with suggestions on what can be improved. This is also a great time to solicit the ideas of the individual and the team to see what they think can be done to improve. You want everyone on the team to be a part of creating success.

Avoid common pitfalls when providing feedback:

- Discuss the *action* and avoid judging the *individual* as a person. This is about behavior.

- Be specific, avoiding exaggeration and generalities.

- Focus on how *you* reacted; don't attribute perspectives to others.

- Include positive feedback as well as negative. Provide a list of what worked and what you liked, then offer insights into areas for improvement. It's helpful to sandwich the feedback and close with positives.

- Don't belabor the point and beat a dead horse.

- Minimize the opportunity for the person to become defensive. Make sure you aren't suggesting they'll be removed from the team if they don't improve. Don't attack the person.

- If the feedback session gets tense, you may be tempted to try to defuse it with humor. Make sure you aren't undermining your own credibility with inappropriate humor.

Seek and Collect Feedback

Time split review: Time each presenter so you have "splits" or individual times for each person. Match this with the slides covered by each person and with general time allotted to each section so you can re-balance. Did you spend too much time on the intro or the closing? Too little on the defense of the strategy? Only by timing each and matching it back to the slides and sections will you know what needs to be adjusted to ensure the most effective presentation.

Slide-by-slide review: The entire team and the coach should go through the full deck slide-by-slide. The goal is twofold: to critique the visuals using the slide checklist as well as the overall flow of the story. Are there any errors on the slides? (Pixelator time!) Does the story make sense? Should slides or sections be re-ordered to create a more effective story? This can be a monotonous process – but it is so worth it.

The team is often too close to the presentation to recognize problems in slides and in the story. Having fresh eyes on the slides will illuminate elements you didn't see before. Rest assured the judges will have picked up on those problems – it is much better to do the slide-by-slide review than have the judges point out problems during a feedback session after you lost the competition.

Measuring Your Performance

It is helpful to use a rubric when evaluating case competition performance. This will bring structure to the assessment, which will help you focus on what is important. Below is a self-evaluation rubric we have adapted from various case competitions.

Business Acumen

Poor – Team demonstrates only a passing knowledge of the issues of the case.

Acceptable – Team demonstrates a good grasp on the issues as presented in the case.

Outstanding – Team demonstrates outside research that goes beyond the facts presented in the case. They have an unusually good grasp of the issues surrounding the case.

Strategic Thought

Poor – Team does not present a compelling rationale for choosing the issues on which they focused their presentation.

Acceptable – Team makes a reasonable case for why they chose the issues on which they focused their presentation.

Outstanding – Team makes an outstanding case for why they chose the issues on which they focused their presentation.

Decision Making

Poor – Team did not demonstrate that they considered a variety of courses of action to address the issue(s) on which they focused.

Acceptable – Team demonstrated they considered more than one course of action to address the issue(s) on which they focused.

Outstanding – Team demonstrated they considered multiple courses of action to address the issue(s) on which they focused.

Analysis

Poor – Team did a poor job of explaining their rationale for their recommended course of action. They failed to provide adequate qualitative and quantitative analytical support for their recommendations. Their thinking and logic were fuzzy.

Acceptable – Team did an acceptable job of explaining their rationale for their recommended course of action. They provided some qualitative and quantitative analytical support for their recommendations. They demonstrated a basic grasp of critical thinking concepts and their application.

Outstanding – Team did an outstanding job of explaining their rationale for their recommended course of action. They provided strong qualitative and quantitative analytical support for their recommendations. They demonstrated an outstanding grasp of critical thinking concepts and their application.

Presentation Effectiveness

Poor – Team's poise, body language, eye contact with judges, and use of language were poor. The presentation lacked clarity and a logical structure.

Acceptable – Team's poise, body language, eye contact with judges, and use of language were adequate. The presentation was clear and followed a logical structure.

Outstanding – Team's poise, body language, eye contact with judges, and use of language were outstanding. Their presentation and logic were compelling.

Responses and Q&A

Poor – Team seemed ill-prepared to answer questions, indicating a poor overall grasp of their ideas and suggestions. They were hesitant in their responses and didn't completely answer the questions.

Acceptable – Team demonstrated a basic overall grasp of their ideas and suggestions. They addressed the questions put to them in an adequate manner.

Outstanding – Team demonstrated an extraordinary grasp of their ideas and suggestions. They anticipated questions and were able to easily answer all of them in a clear, concise, and convincing manner.

Earlier we talked about perfect practice. Debriefing these practice runs and getting constructive feedback based on a structured rubric is an element of perfect practice. Unless you know how judges are receiving your story, you won't know the areas you need to improve. It can be tough, but it is worth it.

Chapter 23: Networking and Sportsmanship

Case competitions offer some terrific networking opportunities – don't neglect this!

Judges

Judging panels comprise predominantly business executives. Many may be from the subject company, and many may be drawn from the network of the host institution. These individuals can be valuable assets to your network.

This may not seem immediately obvious, but you should take every advantage and opportunity to build your network. You never know from where the next opportunity may arise. Many competitions have time and space to network with judges; you may be tired and may not be in the mood, depending on how the competition goes. Just do it.

Other Teams

The other teams in the competition are also a great opportunity to build your network. Yes, they are the competition, and they are probably some of the most driven and successful individuals at the other schools. You want to know them. Networking with the other teams is founded upon sportsmanship, which includes being professional and friendly throughout the competition. Display your best behavior in the snack or break room, in the restrooms and halls of the building where the team rooms are, back at the hotel, on the shuttle, EVERYWHERE, at all times before, during, and after the competition. Be humble in victory, and without bitterness in defeat.

Connecting and Follow-up

Throughout the competition you will come into contact with students, SMEs, judges, and coaches. This is one of the biggest benefits of participating in case competitions. You can capitalize on this opportunity by staying connected with these individuals. Your two best opportunities are collecting business cards and making LinkedIn connections. It is appropriate when you meet people to ask them for business cards so you can stay in contact. Make sure you contact them via email or LinkedIn within a few weeks – sooner is better and late is better than never.

Your initial contact should include two key elements:
- Remind them that you met at the case competition.
- Let them know that it was nice to meet them and speak with them and that you look forward to staying connected.

Pro Tip: Include a specific element of a conversation if you had one. If you did not speak directly with someone (e.g., a judge), it is still okay to contact them via LinkedIn. Also, DO NOT ask this person for a job or a favor. If the connection develops and you build a relationship with the individual, it is okay to ask advice or for feedback. Generally speaking, though, favors should be offered and not asked for upfront. Your goal is to build on the connection.

Case competitions are great – we hope you get by now how much we value the learning that takes place. Yet you will get the most out of the competition only if you capitalize on it by strengthening your network – make use of the opportunity!

CHAPTER 24: BUILDING A WINNING CULTURE AT YOUR SCHOOL

Building a winning culture begins with a committed group of individuals willing to support, encourage, inspire, and push students to realize the benefits inherent in case competitions. Part of the formula is certainly funding. Case competitions can be expensive to attend and most students won't have enough disposable income to fund their participation without assistance from the institution. There are two ways to approach securing funding, and we've seen success with a combination of both.

Funding

First is starting small, finding success, and leveraging that proof of concept to secure more funding. In our first two years, we were providing funding for only one competition per year. The cost was primarily travel within the state, so a rental car and hotels (plus some lunches during prep sessions) amounted to just a couple of thousand dollars. That has grown to four to six fully funded competitions per year and spending of $10K to $12K on participation each year.

A second option is creating your own internal case competition, fully funded by a corporate sponsor. This is a win-win for both the institution and the company. The institution creates an opportunity for more students to participate in a case competition and gain valuable skills. We also enjoyed showcasing our talent to a company in which we want to place our students. For the company, they gain exposure to the students and are able to evaluate talent.

In terms of persuading leadership to invest in the program, we have capitalized over the years on the positive external lift we gained from our success as well as the outstanding value that the students perceive about the school. Know what levers are important to your college to secure funding, and make sure you are collecting data that supports investing in this type of programming. The good news is that case competitions do provide a wealth of learning opportunities for students – so it is a matter of capturing the data and using it intelligently to support them.

Introducing Concepts with Workshops and "Safe" Practice

We introduce case competitions and case analysis from the first week students are on campus. It is an intentional choice to ensure that students know from the beginning that this is an important part of our learning process and how we teach business fundamentals.

From the initial introduction, our goal is to build the skills of the students progressively – we start with education and workshops and then move on to experiential learning where students practice and receive feedback.

Our case workshop series includes the following sessions, and each is required programming for the full-time MBAs:
- Orientation – "What is a case competition and why is it part of our program" and "How to analyze cases"
- Month 1 – "How to Approach and Prepare for Case Competitions"
- Month 2 – "Storytelling and Advanced Presentation Slide Design"
- Month 3 – Practice Case Analysis and Presentation

"Apprentice" Model and Peer Coaching

An important element of building a culture is to leverage more experienced students to mentor and prepare newer students. We do this in a couple of different ways:

Mixing teams for required case competitions: In order to encourage transfer of knowledge from student to student, we mix experienced students with less experienced students during the internal case competition. This also makes the newer students more comfortable because they know they have someone on the team who has a better idea of what to do.

Additionally, we hear from students that asking people to be on your case team is about as comfortable as asking someone out on a date. Therefore, by creating teams for the internal competition, we maximize participation so that students won't have the "I couldn't find a team" excuse.

Using veteran case competition participants as coaches: We do this during the internal competition as well as during the case competition season. These students work with teams to provide insights into time strategy, provide feedback after practice rounds, and simulate Q&A.

This serves several purposes – the students who are coaching provide a great service to the less experienced students, but they are also learning by teaching others. We find that these students perform even better on their own teams. Long term, they are learning skills (like feedback and coaching) that will pay dividends long in the future by improving their management and leadership performance.

Mandatory Fun

One of the most influential things we've done to build a culture of success has been to require participation in our internal case competition. Before the advent of the internal competition, we were successful in preparing a relatively small percentage of our students to perform at the highest level.

We recognized that a lot of students were pretty intimidated by case competitions, and that in order to provide the value to a greater number of students, we were going to have to push them out of the nest in order to show them they could fly. In many respects, the major barrier to entry for case competitions was fear. Therefore, between the programs office and the career office, we banded together to set an expectation that students participate in the internal competition.

Since we did this the first time, we have strengthened our pre-competition preparation in order to make sure the students feel confident going into the competition, but it is the act of flying (and getting feedback) that truly cements the learning process. The true magic is that once they've done it the first time, they are far more likely to try it again. Over the 4-year period since we implemented the required competition, we've progressed from having one or two powerhouse teams to having five distinct teams in one semester that placed 1st or 2nd in five different competitions.

Recognizing Excellence

It is no secret that humans respond to recognition and that culture is built by promoting the behavior you want to see. This holds true for building a culture of success in case competitions. We take every opportunity to highlight the accomplishments of the students. The following are examples:

- We keep the big novelty checks on display in the programs office so that interviewing students see them.

- There is a large trophy display alongside the checks where the entire student body, staff, and prospective students can see them. It is a core conversation topic when we are recruiting students, and a visual reminder when people come into the office for any type of advising, that success in competitions is part of who we are.

- We recognize excellence in case competitions during graduation by having all students who were successful in a competition come to the stage and receive a plaque.

- We lobbied to have one of our most winning teams recognized during halftime of a televised basketball game.

- We invested in a high-end video, highlighting the positive learning outcomes of participating in a case competition featuring another accomplished team. This is shown during each orientation and is posted on our website.

Creating a winning culture is a process that requires a concerted effort of many different stakeholders related to the program. Not only must a program office be involved, but the career office should relate the short-term value and help connect with companies or recruiters to serve as judges.

Faculty should help prepare students for competitions by acting as SMEs, and alumni should act as SMEs and amplify access to others in their own network. The great value of these competitions is that all your stakeholders will be excited to rally around the students.

This creates an opportunity to engage stakeholders in a way that they will enjoy and that will strengthen their relationship with your program.

A culture of winning doesn't happen overnight, and it won't happen in a vacuum. Deciding that you want to create that culture is the first step. Next is building a coalition of individuals around your institution, those who are just as committed as you are. From there, it takes perseverance and patience. You can do it!

CONCLUSION

In the spirit of how we coach students to tell a story, we will now tell you what we told you. We have opened up our winning playbook, one that's proven successful. We've broken the book up into two sections, presentations and the competitions themselves.

A continued theme throughout is simplicity. Keep in mind, though, that creating simplicity takes a good deal more time and effort than complexity. You must be ruthlessly efficient with the time allotted to ensure you are spending time where it will be most effective in order to create a message that is memorable and repeatable. This begins with leading with the answer (your strategy) and continues with backing up your strategy with data and explaining how your strategy will be implemented.

We also want you to keep in mind that if you don't point out the risks in your strategy, someone else will. Be proactive about risk and maintain a solution orientation throughout the presentation. Your goal should be to articulate the strategy in one sentence – and your audience should be able to do the same.

Storyboard to ensure you tell a coherent story and spend the time to design clean slides – particularly when displaying data! Attention to detail in the story and visual representation of the story will make a tremendous difference in how you and your team are perceived. Coupled with outstanding delivery, you have the winning formula for persuading an audience that your idea is the right one.

When your audience starts asking questions, the goal is to be able to say, "I'm glad you asked ... " and then support your answer with a backup slide. This technique will make you appear very well-prepared and competent. The best path forward for being prepared is to capture your research as you go into backup slides and then organize it with the linked Appendix. It is a differentiator – in competitions, yes, but more importantly in your career.

The competitions themselves are environments in which creating the right team is critical because team dynamic is often central to success. You'll be spending a great deal of time training and preparing for the competition – be sure the right mix of individuals is on the team.

You must train like you fight, simulating the competition environment as accurately as possible to ensure you are ready for the real thing. This is important because the competitions themselves are a great simulation for real-world experience – and preparing for the competition is part of preparing for outstanding performance long-term.

To ensure that you spend your time where it will be most effective, develop a plan of attack prior to the competition; establishing a clear working timeline will ensure you stay disciplined and don't end up in distracting rabbit holes. Remember to focus on what is interesting *and* important. Be 100 percent sure you have crossed all your i's and dotted your t's because in the heat of the competition, using a checklist will help ensure you don't miss important details. And re-check that i's and t's sentence because details matter.

During competitions, we have three elements that can be the difference between first and second place. Make sure the right people are presenting each section and that all handoffs are smooth. This includes the Q&A – anticipate the questions the judges will ask and practice responding to the questions to ensure your audience knows that your team has a deep understanding of the proposed solution. When (and that's when, not if) you make it to the second or third round of a competition, stay focused on evaluating your performance and making the necessary adjustments. Sleep when you win.

The crux of ensuring that you and your team are in the best possible position to win the competition is to ensure you are gathering and acting on as much feedback as possible. Keep thinking about the bicycle simile. Feedback is a gift – with it, you know in advance how someone will respond to your idea. Without it you are flying blind.

Take advantage of all the network development these competitions afford you – you won't regret it. Take the time to work with people at your institution who can help you build a case competition program – it will pay dividends later in your career.

Outstanding performance does not happen by mistake. It happens as a result of careful preparation, feedback, and hard work by the team. All of these elements are instrumental to success. This book provides you with the first of these. It will be up to you to solicit and act on the feedback and work your tail off during competitions. When we've compared notes with other programs about their training and preparation regimens, it has become clear to us that we have been successful in large part because of the effort our teams and staff put into the process.

Case competitions are powerful learning tools that drive lessons in critical thinking and analysis, interpersonal skills, teamwork, and influence. Experiential learning, like these case competitions, is the transmission of your business school engine. One must learn how to take the knowledge and skills gained in the classroom and transmit them effectively into action – this is what these competitions build.

We hope you take this as a playbook for maximizing the potential of business school learning at your institution – after all, this isn't just about winning at competitions, it is about capitalizing on your knowledge to be a more forceful and effective business leader.

ABOUT THE AUTHORS

JASON RIFE

Jason is the Director of Graduate Business Career Services at the University of Florida. Before joining UF, he was a strategy consultant for McKinsey & Company and held corporate roles with ExxonMobil and John Deere. For the past five years, Jason has applied his experience with building and communicating recommendations for senior executives toward coaching MBA students on landing top-tier jobs and winning case competitions.

During his time at UF, the full-time MBA program has made record gains in placement rates and starting salaries. In 2016 the program was ranked #2 globally in Student Assessment of Career Services by *The Economist*. UF MBA Case Competition teams have amassed 16 first-place wins since 2013 with Kara and Jason as co-coaches. Jason earned his MBA from Duke University and his bachelor's from Texas Tech University.

KARA KRAVETZ CUPOLI

Kara is the Director of the Full-Time MBA program at UNC's Kenan-Flagler Business School, overseeing all aspects of the full-time MBA program. Prior to her role at UNC Chapel Hill, Kara spent 18 years at the University of Florida, most recently as the Senior Director of Full-Time Student Affairs & MBA Engagement. As part of this role, she coached case competition teams for over a decade.

Kara and Jason developed a proven and repeatable method of preparing successful MBA case competition teams for the UF MBA program. This success led not only to a stunning number of competition victories, but also to increased student satisfaction with the program and improved performance in their post-MBA careers.

Kara recently earned her PhD from the University of Florida; her dissertation focused on predicting placement of MBA students and the linkages among personality, participation in professional development, and placement success. She also holds an MS from Florida State University and a BA from the Pennsylvania State University.

MARC COSENTINO

Marc Cosentino is the CEO of CaseQuestions.com and the author of several best-selling books on consulting.

For almost three decades Cosentino's work has towered over the field of case interviews. He has advised and coached more than 100,000 students.

Case in Point is now published in four languages and was called the "MBA Bible" by *The Wall Street Journal.* It has been the best-selling case prep book on the planet for the last ten-plus years and the number one consulting book and number two interview book worldwide for more than seven years.

Cosentino travels internationally presenting case workshops at 45 schools annually, training students on answering case questions and training career services professionals on giving case interviews. He consults with and designs cases for private sector firms, government agencies, and non-profit organizations. Cosentino is a graduate of Harvard's Kennedy School and the University of Denver.

Photo: Martha Stewart 2005

Additional Products by CaseQuestions.com

Books available on amazon.com

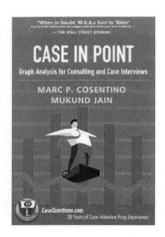

CaseQuestions Interactive
Online Training: Math Drills, Market Sizing,
Case Starts, Videos and 12 full cases
How to Answer a Case Question
Going Beyond the Expected Answer –
5 hours of online training

CaseQuestions.com

15 Videos: Case starts and full cases with commentary

Printed in Great Britain
by Amazon